TOP WRECK DIVES OF THE WORLD

TOP
WRECK
DIVES
OF THE WORLD

CONTRIBUTING EDITOR
JACK JACKSON

NH
NEW
HOLLAND

First published in 2007 by
New Holland Publishers (UK) Ltd
London • Cape Town • Sydney • Auckland

Garfield House, 86–88 Edgware Road
London, W2 2EA, United Kingdom
www.newhollandpublishers.com

80 McKenzie Street, Cape Town, 8001 South Africa
66 Gibbes Street, Chatswood, NSW 2067 Australia
218 Lake Road, Northcote, Auckland New Zealand

ISBN 978 1 84537 466 2

Publishing Manager: Clare Hubbard
Design: bluegumdesigners.com
Cartography: Stephen Dew
Picture research: Joanne Forrest-Smith
Production: Marion Storz

Reproduction by Pica Digital Pte Ltd, Singapore
Printed by Tien Wah Press Pte Ltd, Singapore

10 9 8 7 6 5 4 3 2 1

Disclaimer
The authors and publisher have made every effort to
ensure that all the information given in this book is
accurate at the time of going to press, but they accept no
responsibility for any injury or inconvenience sustained by
any person using this book. Diving is an adventurous sport
so it must be treated with respect.

**Page 1: The huge, encrusted starboard propellor of
the *Umbria* is clear of the coral, Wingate Reefs, Port
Sudan.**
**Page 2: A diver about to penetrate the MV *Giannis D*
on Sha'b Abu Nuhâs, Egypt.**

ABOUT THE CONTRIBUTING EDITOR AND AUTHORS

Diver, mountaineer, photographer, lecturer and author, **JACK JACKSON** has travelled
the remote areas of the world since 1967, both privately and as leader of scientific and
cultural expeditions. Originally an industrial chemist in the oil and photographic film
industries, he found the call of adventure too strong and exchanged it for a life as
expedition leader, lecturer and photographer. He draws on several decades of experience
of diving in many parts of the world, has intimate knowledge of diving the Red Sea and
Pacific Ocean, and ran a dive boat in the Sudan for 12 years.

ANDY AND ANGIE BELCHER are a professional, award-winning writing and
photography team. They specialize in action, adventure and outdoor locations throughout
the world. Their work has appeared in many of the world's top travel and adventure
magazines as well as *AA Spiral Travel Guides* and *Berlitz Travel Guides*. They have produced
over 50 children's books, many with marine- and adventure-based themes. Andy specializes
in photography of hard-to-reach places, spending most of 2006 either underwater or
underground! Examples of their work can be found at www.andybelcher.com

BOB HALSTEAD learned to dive in 1968. In 1973 he moved to Papua New Guinea
and, with his diver wife, formed the first full-time sport diving business there. An
underwater photographer, Bob won the Australasian Underwater Photographer of the
Year Award in 1983. Bob has led sport diving, filming and scientific expeditions, and has
discovered several marine species new to science. He has published eight books as well as
hundreds of magazine articles on diving and marine life.

JASON MARTIN has always loved the ocean. Having been a diver in the navy, he left to
become a diving instructor and travel the world. His work took him to the west coast of
Africa, the Caribbean, the Mediterranean and Bermuda. Returning to South Africa he
started diving with Wreckseekers and the National Survey of Underwater Heritage. He
also filmed the wrecks off Robben Island. Jason has now started the Frog Squad, a
professional marine and commercial diving service to the film industry.

ROCHELLE MUTTON, a journalist since 1996, first developed a niche in diving and
marine science reporting along the vast western Australian coast in 2000. She traversed the
state's coastline and its islands, working with leading marine photographers Peter and
Margy Nicholas to capture the delights and latest science from under the sea. Together
they supplied breaking news and feature packages to Australian newspapers for three
years. In September 2004 she relocated to Johannesburg, South Africa, where she
freelanced foreign news for international broadcasters and newspapers. She is currently
alternating her reporting between London newsrooms and the raw issues and great
outdoors of southern Africa.

LAWSON WOOD is from Eyemouth in Scotland and has been scuba-diving since 1965.
Now with over 15,000 dives logged in all of the world's oceans, he is the author and co-
author of over 40 books. He is a founding member of the Marine Conservation Society
and founder of the first marine nature reserve in Scotland. He made photographic history
in the UK by becoming the first person to gain Fellowships with the Royal Photographic
Soceity and British Institute of Professional Photographers solely for underwater
photography. A Fellow of the Royal Geographical Society, he has been presented with
many awards for outstanding marine conservation and underwater photography.

CONTENTS

INTRODUCTION By Jack Jackson

Wreck diving is one of the most fascinating and popular types of diving worldwide. It is particularly popular in temperate waters where visibility often makes wreck diving the most interesting available. A combination of wars, bad weather and human error has left thousands of wrecks, particularly from the World War I and II. More ships are thought to have sunk around the coasts of the UK than any other country in the world with the best estimate being over 250,000.

The word 'wreck' is an attraction in itself for most divers. The mind ponders on the wreck's history, the manner, drama and horror of the sinking, how and when it was rediscovered and the thought of possible treasure – whether that be old enough to be of archaeological importance, have monetary value or be just a souvenir of the wreck. For marine archaeologists underwater wrecks are time capsules preserving moments in time. For marine biologists wrecks are living laboratories where they can study organisms' development and lifestyles from when they first arrive on what is essentially a blank canvas.

Even if the memory of a ship's sinking fades or is forgotten altogether, most wrecks remain on the seabed for hundreds of years. There is the joy of swimming along decks, the bridge, companionways and open holds that are now colonized with attractive and often colourful marine life and, with the necessary skills, a diver can penetrate the interior. For underwater photographers, wrecks are a challenge to their photographic skill in capturing the mood, combining the light filtering down from the surface with the only subjects underwater that have straight lines – ideal for framing pictures.

There are many reasons why wrecks end up underwater and most of them are tragic: conflicts resulting in sea battles, torpedoed merchant ships and the dumping of surplus machinery; rogue waves; poor loading or shifting cargo in a rough sea; collisions with other vessels or floating objects such as icebergs or lost cargo-carrying containers; piracy, which still occurs today; scuttling; storms; tsunamis; mechanical and structural failure; navigational error; insurance fraud; and human error, including intoxicated captains.

Today there are millions of vessels navigating the seas, lakes and rivers and aircraft flying over them yet, despite modern hi-tech equipment, wrecks still occur. The charts are not foolproof; they are often based on old information and only updated accurately around ports. Some large reefs in the Red Sea were not marked on many charts when I ran a boat there and, recently, a British warship and an American submarine have hit rocks.

In recent years ships, aeroplanes, tracked and other vehicles have been environmentally cleaned and made 'safe for sport divers' before being intentionally sunk as artificial reefs to attract more diving tourism.

The story of a ship does not stop with its sinking. Erosion starts immediately and masts and other spars that were not broken during the sinking soon are. Wrecks that occur in violent waters soon break up, but many sink in waters where they remain almost intact. A wreck is often the only thing standing up from a large area of seabed so it becomes a rich habitat for marine creatures, from sessile organisms like anemones, corals and sponges, through slow-moving ones like shellfish and sea stars to fish hunting, hiding or taking shelter. Fishermen find that wrecks are great places to find fish.

There are instances where very old wooden wrecks have been preserved because they were lying in water that lacks oxygen and the marine worms that destroy wood but, in general, wooden wrecks break

USING THIS BOOK

MAPS
Each map has a key, clearly explaining what the symbols mean. The actual position of the wreck is denoted by the number in the red circle.

DESTINATION DIRECTORY
For each destination there is concise travel, weather and safety information, including locations of recompression (hyperbaric) chambers on pages 154–8.

Opposite: Ship's telegraph encrusted with marine life on the *Shinkoku Maru*, Chuuk (Truk) Lagoon.

up relatively quickly, becoming fragile and dangerous to divers. Metal wrecks last much longer but even these will eventually break up and become dangerous. From a diver's point of view, metal wrecks are most interesting when they have been underwater for about 50 years – enough time to achieve a healthy coverage of marine life but not long enough for corrosion to render them unstable. In most cases, wrecks situated in the open sea will be draped with lost fishing nets.

Ships stranded on rocks or the shoreline are gradually broken up by wave action and, if dangerous to shipping or causing pollution, may be blown up by the authorities. Ships that hit a reef often sit on the edge of the reef for years, but then slide off into deep water during a storm. An example of this is the *Jolanda/Yolanda* on Shark Reef at Egypt's Râs Muhammad.

Sometimes inclement weather can improve on the work of man. In 1992 the then largest intentionally sunk ship in the world, the *Spiegel Grove* (see page 28) off Key Largo, Florida, failed to sink at the first attempt, and when finally it was sunk it ended up on its starboard side instead of on its keel as planned. However, in 2005 a combination of currents scouring out an empty space beneath the vessel and strong surge from Hurricane Dennis caused it to roll upright.

Throughout history wrecks in shallow water have been profitable for divers and many ingenious 'machines', including the equivalent of the modern diving bell, were manufactured from leather, wood and metal to facilitate the recovery of valuable cargo. By the 18th century primitive diving helmets with air pumped from the surface were in use. However, it was the development of Self-contained Underwater Breathing Apparatus (SCUBA), which freed the diver of hoses supplying air from the surface, that made it easy for sport divers to dive on wrecks. Until recently, divers often dived to depths that were dangerous on air in order to reach wrecks. However, today amateur technical divers use techniques developed by cave divers in Florida, which enable them to descend beyond 70m (230ft) using Trimix, and to return safely to the surface using different decompression gas mixes on the ascent.

While the use of SCUBA has facilitated scientific study of the underwater domain, it has also brought more treasure hunters searching for junks loaded with Ming porcelain or galleons containing gold and silver. Several divers and governments have made fortunes – to the detriment of historical records, because a proper archaeological survey of a wreck can tell us so much more about the lives of the crew. While detailed underwater archaeological excavation began in the Mediterranean Sea, excavations like that of the *Mary Rose* in the UK did not give up just cannons, but also bows and arrows, clothing, footwear, navigational and medical instruments and much more. This allowed the experts to piece together a detailed picture of how the crew lived at the time of the sinking. Over four million people have since visited the raised wreck. Many countries are now making laws to stop the indiscriminate plunder of ancient vessels.

The United Nations Educational, Scientific and Cultural Organization (UNESCO) believes that more than three million wrecks lie beneath the world's oceans. Many of these attract professional treasure hunters who use increasingly advanced technology to pillage them systematically.

For many years some divers' main reason for diving on shipwrecks was to remove objects like the bell, the binnacle or other brass objects as mementoes or for monetary gain. However, there are so many divers now that this cannot continue, and there is a feeling that things should be left where they are for future divers to enjoy. In the UK if divers remove material from a wreck and then sell it for profit, they are deemed to be diving for reward, so they must conduct their dives in strict accordance with Health and Safety Executive (HSE) regulations.

This acts as a deterrent because it involves licensing and a more detailed and expensive diving medical.

Faced with laws full of loopholes, several organizations, working with UNESCO, are drawing up an international convention to preserve the underwater cultural heritage. Defined as 'all traces of human existence having a cultural, historical or archaeological character, which have been partially or totally underwater, periodically or continuously, for at least 100 years', the convention covers more than wrecks. There are worries that the wording is too 'all-encompassing' – treating all shipwrecks over 100 years old as an archaeological resource only. This means that the convention could be used against responsible sport divers and fishermen and it does not necessarily protect military vessels or wrecks in international waters.

Several governments have brought out their own laws to stop divers from plundering wrecks and with some governments a similar situation applies over 'war graves' – 'protected shipwrecks or aircraft on which lives were lost as the result of military action' – as a mark of respect to surviving relatives of the people lost (see page 15).

It should be remembered that many wrecks actually have owners who may or may not intend to salvage the vessels. They may be the original owner, such as the Ministry of Defence or the shipping line, the insurance company that paid out on it, someone who bought the wreck for salvage purposes or even a diving club whose members now have the right to dive on it.

Some wrecks are designated as dangerous and may be marked as such on the charts: they may have been carrying explosives or dangerous chemicals, or their structures may be fragile and thought likely to collapse. In these cases it is wise to take note of local diving knowledge – many wrecks carrying explosives are dived by thousands of divers every year. The important thing is not to touch anything. Each diver is responsible for his or her own safety. Never allow overconfidence or peer pressure to sway good judgement. Diving at depth is more dangerous than diving in shallower water, and incidents are more likely to be serious. The further the dive goes beyond mainstream sport diving limits, the more risk the diver must accept. No amount of training or equipment will eliminate risk completely.

FIRST RESEARCH THE WRECK

Details on how to research a wreck that has not yet been found would fill a book in itself, so in this title we are concentrating on known wrecks. There is no shortage of books, articles, websites and even films on the better-known wrecks. However, they are not always accurate on the story behind the sinking – the old adage 'never let the truth get in the way of a good story' may apply in some cases. In the developed world, wreck lists supplied by government agencies such as the Hydrographic Office and dive training agencies should be accurate on the actual position and depth of the wreck and any restrictions to diving on it.

Some wrecks are marked with buoys attached to permanent shot lines and many wrecks are marked on charts, but in the Third World you cannot rely on charts. If a wreck is not marked, divers will need to know either its latitude and longitude, so that they can use a Global Positioning System (GPS) receiver to get to this position, or its transits (see page 10). Either of these will bring you close enough to see the wreck underwater or locate it by searching in a grid pattern with an echo sounder – a device that detects changes in the depth of the seabed by timing how long a high-frequency sound takes to echo back to it.

LATITUDE AND LONGITUDE

Parallels of latitude are lines drawn parallel to the equator. The equator is known as 0 degrees, the North Pole as 90°N and the South Pole 90°S. Parallels of latitude indicate distance north or south of the equator.

TONS/TONNES
The weight of a ship, or displacement tonnage (in tonnes) is not used much in commercial shipping. More important is the weight of the estimated volume of the cargo or room for passengers. A number of different tonnage definitions used to exist for calculating port and canal charges, taxation, and so on. Different countries used either the imperial or metric system, but it was also industry practice to measure a large portion of the world's vessels in entirely different ways. The way ships' capacities were given over the years was not consistent and cannot be directly converted between imperial and metric values, so in this book the original ton or tonne used by the owner has been retained.

Meridians of longitude are drawn vertically around the world, with all of them intersecting at the geographical North and South Poles. There are 360 lines, all separated by one degree. By international agreement, the meridian running through Greenwich in London, England, is the prime meridian 0 degrees. Longitude gives an angular distance east or west of the Greenwich meridian to 180 degrees east or west on the other side of the globe.

Normally in each case degrees are divided into 60 minutes (indicated with a number followed by ') and minutes are further divided into 60 seconds (a number followed by ") but electronic navigational systems tend to use decimal values – mostly degrees and decimal minutes.

TRANSITS OR MARKS

If the wreck is lying within sight of the shore, you can use its transits to find it. These allow you to take compass bearings that line up two or more fixed features. Each transit lines up easily visible, fixed features, such as lighthouses, tall buildings, church steeples or some kind of natural feature. Where these lines of sight intersect you are on the position of the site that you are looking for. The wider the angle between the alignment of the bearings, the more accurate the result.

GLOBAL POSITIONING SYSTEM (GPS)

The modern way to locate a wreck that does not have any obvious features above water is to use a GPS receiver. The US Military have placed 24 NAVSTAR satellites plus four spare ones in orbit 20,000km (12,400 miles) above the earth, with each one transmitting its precise position and correct time. GPS receivers must have a direct line of sight to the satellites and must be locked on to the signals from at least three satellites to calculate a two-dimensional latitude and longitude position. (With signals from four or more satellites, the receiver can also determine the user's altitude.) Once the user's

position has been determined, a GPS receiver can calculate other information, such as speed, bearing, track, trip distance, distance to destination, and even sunrise and sunset time.

The more satellite fixes, the more accurate the position. This is mainly because the quartz clock in the GPS receiver is less accurate than those of the satellites, so the GPS receiver recalculates the fixes until they converge on a single point, then corrects its own clock setting. By correcting for internal clock errors and the time it has taken to receive each signal, a GPS receiver can compute its own latitude and longitude down to about 5m (16ft). In times of conflict the American military can move some of the satellites to gain more accuracy in the theatre of conflict or turn them off altogether – so a European system is planned.

Keep in mind that anything that relies on batteries or electronics can go wrong and is subject to operator error.

DIVING SAFELY

Wrecks can break up or be snagged with fishing lines, fishing nets and baggage nets, making them dangerous. Any diver can enjoy diving around a wreck, but a course in wreck diving is strongly recommended before attempting to penetrate large wrecks.

Wrecks are sharp places so a dual system of buoyancy is recommended: either a dry suit plus a BCD or a dual-bladder or wing-type BCD. Wear gloves for protection from sharp metal. A spare low-volume mask can be carried in a pocket.

Carry a sharp knife and a suitable monofilament line cutter or shears for cutting monofilament fishing line and nets. Most divers strap their diving knife to one of their legs, but in this position it can be dislodged by the safety guideline or tangled up in fishing lines or nets. Have a separate smaller knife attached to one arm or inside a BCD pocket where it can easily be reached.

If possible dive at slack water. If there is a current, quickly descend the shot line to get into the lee of the wreck. In bad visibility a further safety guideline from the bottom of the shot line to or along the wreck may be necessary. If there is not a fixed shot line, the first pair of divers onto the wreck should tie off the shot line and the final pair of divers to ascend should release it. Take extra care on wooden wrecks, which may collapse.

As with caves, serious penetration requires backup equipment (redundancy). Large single scuba cylinders with two separate regulators on an 'H' or 'Y'-valve or twin scuba cylinders connected by a manifold with a centre isolation valve and two separate regulators, one on each scuba cylinder valve.

Have a good underwater dive-light and carry at least one other powered by disposable alkaline batteries (which lose their charge gradually and won't suddenly leave you in the dark) as backup. A narrow beam will minimize backscatter from particulate matter in poor visibility. Some wreck divers fit small lights to hard helmets to leave their hands free, but in very bad visibility the light can reflect straight back into your eyes. Twist-on type lights may switch on as the increased pressure squeezes the casing on descent, so check these often throughout the dive. Make sure that all equipment is streamlined against your body to minimize the possibility of snagging; if necessary, use bungee cord. When penetrating a shipwreck, keep an eye on your depth – if the ship has settled into a soft seabed, the interior may be deeper than the exterior.

Exhaust bubbles, fins, hands and the diver's wake disturb sediment, which can quickly reduce visibility to zero. It is also easy to get lost in a confusion of companionways. For those reasons it is very dangerous to penetrate a wreck without some foolproof method of return to a clear exit point. Tie off a safety guideline outside the wreck before penetrating, feed it out as you go and tie back any doors or hatches so that they cannot close in a

Left: Bright red sponges are very common among the ribs of the *Umbria* wreck, Wingate Reefs, Port Sudan.

Countries using the metric system refer to scuba cylinders by their internal water capacity in litres and their working pressure in bars. Countries using the imperial system refer to cylinders by their gas capacity in cubic feet at full working pressure. It is not a direct conversion of volume from litres to cubic feet.

change of current. The line should have some tension, but not so much that it could be severed by sharp edges; it should have reliable tie-off points; and it should not have to be crossed over because it must be easily followed in zero visibility by letting it run through the fingers.

Wrecks that have been specifically sunk for divers should have had all doors and hatches either welded shut or removed. Use the rule of thirds on breathing gas supply: turn around when one-third of the breathing gas is used up, leaving one-third for finding the way out and back to the surface, and one-third for emergencies.

Bend the knees 90 degrees to keep them away from the bottom. Moving the fins from the knees or the ankles (flutter kick), instead of from the hip, can minimize the amount of silt stirred up by the fins. Another method is a frog kick. When moving through hatchways or narrow passageways, pull with the fingers and glide, but watch for sharp edges.

DIVING ON DEEPER WRECKS

The definition of deep diving within recreational diving limits on normal compressed air varies with the training agency and the country. Some agencies quote depths deeper than 30m (100ft), while divers trained by European training agencies consider dives in the 30–50m (100–165ft) range to be feasible for advanced divers.

Deep dives require careful planning. Spare full scuba cylinders should be fitted with regulators and attached to the shot line at the depths of any planned decompression stops. Backup divers, who have not dived (so that they do not have any nitrogen already in their tissues if they are called upon to help the divers in the water), should be kitted-up on the boat.

Diving deep on compressed air is hazardous. Nowadays, for wrecks deeper than 50m (165ft), divers are expected to be fully trained in technical diving using Trimix or Heliox. Travel gas mixtures and decompression gas mixtures are carried in

several back- and side-mounted cylinders of different gas mixtures. Alternatively, a closed-circuit rebreather is used. Final decompression can take a long time. Where possible, there should be extra cylinders of decompression gases high on the shot line for safety. However, a floating decompression platform under the boat can be used where currents are strong or the wreck is in a busy shipping lane. Some divers like to use powered underwater scooters on deep wrecks so that they can accomplish more in the allowed bottom time.

ANIMALS AND PLANTS LIVING IN, ON AND AROUND WRECKS

The types of marine organism living on a wreck depend on the geographical location, depth, strength of currents, water temperature and salinity. Any fuel oil or other toxic substance leaking out will kill most organisms. So long as it is not too deep, a wreck will act just like a coral reef, but with even more and larger hidey-holes where marine creatures can shelter from currents or hide. It provides a substrate on which larvae can settle and thrive. There will be some permanently resident large fish that live entirely on the smaller ones using the wreck as shelter. The fish and plankton in turn attract larger pelagic fish that prey on them. In general, wrecks are colourful places if lit with an underwater light, and are perfect for macro and fish photography.

PHOTOGRAPHY

Macro and fish photography on wrecks will be the same as they are anywhere underwater except that photographers will be spoilt for choice on subjects. Getting good wide-angle shots is more difficult. Photographers should have the widest angle lens and largest dome port they can afford to reduce the amount of water between the camera and the subject. Most wreck photographers use a 16mm fisheye lens, but I prefer a 17mm rectilinear lens or the Nikonos 15mm lens to keep the straight lines straight. They

Above: Due to the materials used in their construction, aircraft wrecks such as this Bristol Beaufighter corrode away more quickly than most shipwrecks.

also require large flash guns (strobes). For portrait-type shots make sure that no flash gun or dangling equipment appears in the frame. Wide-angle photographers need to be in place when most suspended particles have had time to settle – where possible before any other divers stir up the sediment with their movements and exhaust bubbles. In the tropics this usually means being the first on the

wreck in the early morning – 07:00 is a good compromise between the clearest visibility and enough ambient light for moody pictures. Photographers should be careful not to disturb the sediment themselves.

An independent slave-operated flash gun can be hidden within the creative scene and triggered by the main flash guns. There will always be some sediment in the water so fit long arms on the flash guns and be careful with aiming them to avoid backscatter. In temperate waters divers may have a very short period of slack water between tides. It also presents more problems with suspended particles, which may cause automatic focus systems to hunt continuously for focus. This will make manual focus necessary, particularly on wide-angle lenses. A dash of fluorescent paint on the most-used focus points on the lens barrel can help with lining up the focus positions when the light is poor.

Very wide-angle shots are better without a flash, relying only on fast film or a high ISO number on digital cameras. Special colour-correction filters are available to correct the colour of underwater shots taken with available light and these can be particularly effective with video and digital still cameras. If the shot can be taken from a position where the photographer can steady the camera on a tripod so as to use long exposures without flash, the tripod can be weighted down with an extra weight belt. The best for underwater work is an antique one made of wood with brass fittings, but whatever type of tripod you use, soak it in freshwater after every dive. For very deep wrecks, the underwater camera system must be rated for the depth envisaged.

Digital cameras allow more pictures per dive than the limit of 36 frames on a 35mm film. The results can be viewed underwater and the subject re-photographed if necessary. However, for publication there are advantages in having the higher resolution of a scanned slide.

Taking video is much easier because videographers have fewer camera controls to operate and can mostly work without additional light, so backscatter is less of a problem.

Where currents and/or long decompression are involved, make sure that your whole camera outfit can be attached to your BCD or harness.

CODE OF CONDUCT

In many countries various dive training agencies and boat operators have voluntary codes of conduct for diving on wrecks. The basics of these are:

- Get the appropriate training before you penetrate a wreck.
- Practise safe, responsible and legal diving. Look after yourself and look after the environment, so that the wreck will still be there for future divers.
- Research the wreck before you dive on it, including ownership and whether it is safe or protected by laws, such as the Protection of Wrecks Act of 1973 or the Protection of Military Remains Act of 1986. Seek official permission where necessary. Do not dive on a designated wreck site without the correct licence.
- Tell someone on shore where you are going and when they should expect you to return.
- Do not damage marine life or the wreck; wrecks provide a habitat for marine life which destructive diving or careless anchoring can ruin. Where available, use fixed shot lines. If you need to use your own line or anchor, ensure that they are secured off the wreck where possible. Use safe diving techniques that will not spoil the wreck for other divers, whatever their interest.
- Do not remove anything as a souvenir – wrecks are part of our maritime history and should be preserved.
- In some countries it is your duty to report your find when you remove and land an artefact. In the UK, this would be to the Receiver of Wreck (see opposite). Finders who act legally and report their finds may be entitled to keep their find or claim a salvage award.
- Avoid handling and raising munitions, including detonators. If disturbed the ordnance may become explosive or have an impact on the marine environment. Munitions containing white phosphorus may ignite spontaneously with the oxygen in moist air.

WHAT IS WRECK?
Wreck is flotsam, jetsam, derelict and lagan found in or on the shores of the sea or any tidal water. It includes ships and aeroplanes, parts of these, and their cargo and equipment. Flotsam is goods and wreckage from a sunken vessel, which are recoverable because they remain afloat. Jetsam is goods or equipment cast overboard in order to lighten a vessel that is in danger of sinking. Derelict is property, whether the vessel or cargo, which has been abandoned and deserted at sea by those who were in charge of it. Lagan is goods and wreckage on the sea bed, and is sometimes buoyed to permit recovery.

WAR GRAVES

War graves are the last resting place of those lost while defending their country and should be left in peace. It is an offence to intrusively dive on a war grave or remove any material from it. This includes the debris field – the trail of wreckage that comes away from the main body of the wreck during the sinking process. This trail can consist of parts of the ship, the cargo and the crew's personal possessions.

Treat war graves as sensitively as you would any other cemetery. Divers are welcome to visit on a look-but-do-not-touch basis, but may not enter such wrecks.

HISTORIC WRECKS

Generally, a wreck over 100 years old is considered historic. Remember that historic wrecks are heritage. In most countries divers may visit and even work on these wrecks, but only if they have the appropriate licence.

THE RECEIVER OF WRECK

All property found in the sea, or washed ashore from tidal water, is owned by someone. Several countries have a Receiver of Wreck. The law in the UK requires finders to report all recoveries to the Receiver of Wreck, however unimportant they may seem; even if you own the wreck from which the material was taken or if it is recovered from another country. The Receiver of Wreck will try to trace an owner so that they can be given the opportunity to claim their property. If no owner is found, or if the owner is willing to waive their rights, the finder may be offered the artefact in lieu of salvage. If the owners are identified and wish to claim their property, the legitimate finder is entitled to a salvage award.

If wreck material remains unclaimed for a year, it usually becomes the property of the Crown. The Receiver of Wreck will then dispose of the material in the most appropriate manner. Each case is judged individually and the Receiver of Wreck makes the final decision on disposal.

In the UK, legitimate finders cannot lose; they either keep the property or receive the net proceeds of the sale. However, the penalties for failing to report the item are severe: the finder forfeits the rights to any salvage, can be fined heavily and is also liable to pay the owner double the value of the property. Take nothing but pictures, leave nothing but bubbles.

Below: The USS *Spiegel Grove* is prepared for sinking as an artificial reef.

ATLANTIC OCEAN

CANADA – Bell Island

By Lawson Wood

Known primarily for the production of iron ore, Bell Island was the main supplier of ore to the Allies during the war. However, its real claim to notoriety comes from a couple of brief but costly encounters with German U-Boats in 1942. Newfoundland became the only place in North America that experienced a direct attack on land by the Nazis. On two separate occasions U-Boats stole into Conception Bay, sinking two ore carriers on each occasion and blowing up the pier on Bell Island.

Opposite: A diver inspecting a large anchor.

SS SAGANAGA ❸

In September 1942, the U-513 commanded by Rolf Ruggenberg made its way undetected into the massive, deep inlet of Conception Bay. On the night of 5 September she struck with deadly force and sank the SS *Saganaga* and the SS *Lord Strathcona* before escaping into open waters and the safety of the North Atlantic. The 125m (410ft) iron ore carrier SS *Saganaga* had a gross tonnage of 5,454 tonnes and was at anchor in Lance Cove when she was struck. Now lying in 34m (112ft) on an even keel, her main deck is at 23m (75ft). There is a gaping hole amidships. This wreck, like the other three in this cove, has suffered top damage by the occasional iceberg that drifts through the sound and gets snared on the superstructure. Imagine a dive on a nearly intact ship from World War II with an iceberg on its deck stretching to the surface!

SS LORD STRATHCONA ❹

The 7,335 tonne, 140m (459ft) SS *Lord Strathcona* was torpedoed on same night as the *Saganaga* and now lies in 36m (118ft) with her main deck at 27m (89ft). This ship requires several dives just to explore the upper deck. Better preserved than the *Saganaga*, the main superstructure is completely open and easily negotiated. The only problem is the time-to-depth limitation. All the holds are open and, with care, the inside of the ship can be explored. There are some fishing nets snagged onto the structure so, as always, care should be taken.

SS ROSE CASTLE ❶

Two months later, on 2 November 2nd, the U-518, under the command of Captain Friedrich Wissmann, entered Conception Bay as a slight detour to Quebec where it offloaded a spy. With the knowledge of the U-513's earlier success, Wissmann approached Lance Cove and sank two more ore carriers, the SS *Rose Castle* and the PLM *27*. The 7,803 tonne, 140m (459ft) *Rose Castle* lies in 40m (131ft) of water,

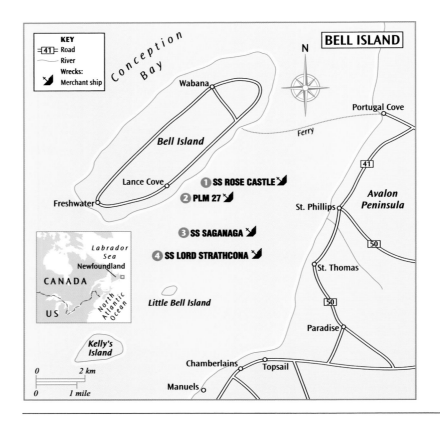

making it the deepest of all the wrecks. The ship is upright, making her upper decks, at around 28m (92ft), perfect for exploration. Due to the depth, the ship is much more intact than any of the others and is considered the best preserved.

PLM 27 ❷

The last of the four ships off Bell Island is the 5,633 tonne, 123m (404ft) PLM *27*, a Free French ore carrier. The initials PLM stand for 'Paris Lyon Marseilles', and she is the most accessible of all the ships. The deck is in only 20m (66ft), but she has sustained the most iceberg damage. Her propeller and rudder are intact and make a fantastic backdrop.

All four ore carriers are possibly the best World War II-era ships I have dived on in cold water, and that certainly includes all those in Scapa Flow, Scotland (see page 57). The water temperature ranges from just above 0°C (32°F) at the seabed to 14°C

(57°F) at the surface – quite a change and certainly a welcome relief as you hang out on the mooring line on the way back to the boat.

These northern Atlantic waters are very similar to British waters in terms of the marine life to be seen; there are species of kelp, bladder wracks, winkles and huge scallops. The wrecks are absolutely smothered in Plumose Anemones and soft corals, with every bit of metal space covered. Lumpsuckers are found all year round and commercially harvested for the roe that is exported to the Baltic States. The sea stars and most nudibranchs are of the same type as those found in British waters, and even the wolf fish are the same. But the wolf fish in these northern waters compete in the ugly stakes with the ocean pout (*Macrozoarces americanus*). This is a type of common eelpout that has grown to massive proportions and is usually over a metre (40 inches) long, with a similar-sized head to the wolf fish, but no teeth!

There are hundreds of flounders all over the seabed, which is also home to sand dollars (a type of flat sea urchin) and large moon snails. Skate are common in shallow waters, and the predominant local species of fish is undoubtedly a local variation of the wrasse family called a 'cunner' (*Tautoglabrus adspersus*). Cod are everywhere, since there is no commercial fishing allowed for this species without a licence to catch individual fish.

Diving really does not get much better than this: the lure of snorkelling with whales, combined with icebergs and pristine World War II wrecks, is just spectacular.

Below: The Radio Room/Marconi Room on the wreck of the SS *Rose Castle*.

UNITED STATES OF AMERICA – East Coast

By Jack Jackson

WRECKS FEATURED

- ★SS ANDREA DORIA
- ★USS ALGOL
- ★MV STOLT DAGALI
- ★WRECKS OFF CAPE HATTERAS
- ★SS PROTEUS
- ★U-352
- ★USCG BIBB
- ★USCG DUANE
- ★USS SPIEGEL GROVE

The East Coast of the USA is one of the most active Scuba-diving areas. Often bathed by the clear, warm waters of the Gulf Stream there is an amazing collection of shipwrecks from Spanish galleons to vessels sunk specifically as artificial reefs. In 1942 the commander of Germany's U-boat fleet, Admiral Karl Donitz, sent five U-boats to attack shipping directly off the East Coast. The USA was unprepared for this onslaught and German U-boats sank nearly 300 vessels while losing very few submarines themselves. Surface conditions can be rough and the currents strong, so a number of the wrecks are only suitable for very experienced divers. For many years, experienced divers regularly endured nitrogen narcosis while diving on wrecks and going much deeper than they should have on air. It was these divers together with the cave-diving community in Florida that were at the forefront in developing what we now know as technical diving.

Opposite: The USCG *Duane* is well covered in corals.

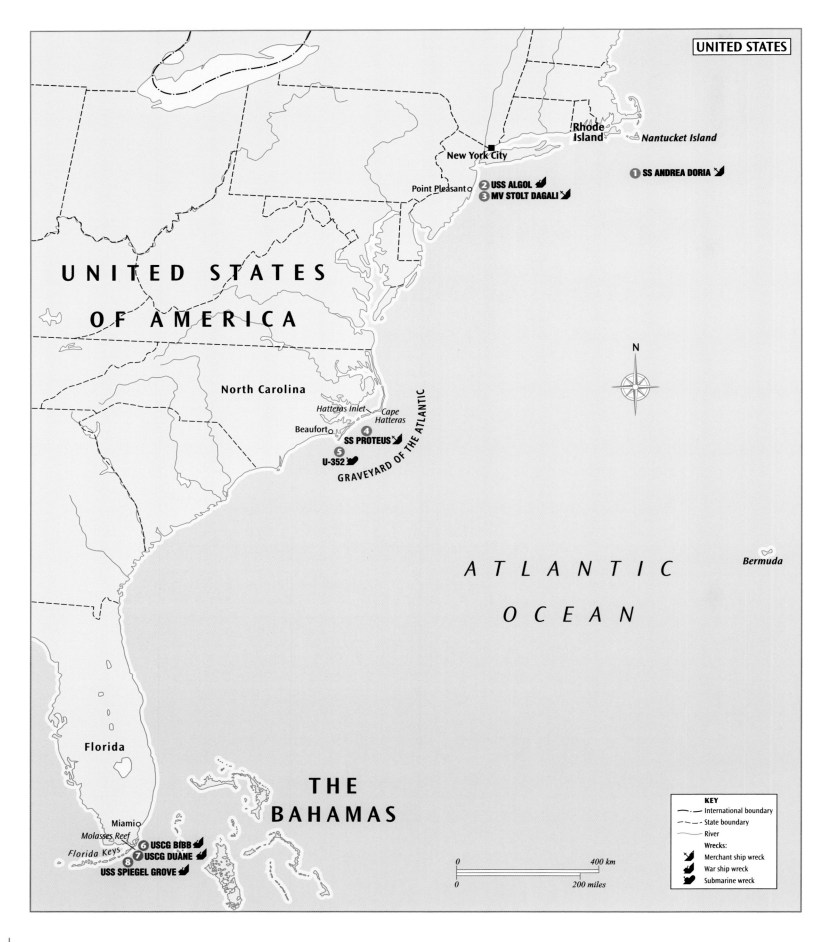

UNITED STATES

Rhode
Island

Nantucket Island

New York City

1 SS ANDREA DORIA

Point Pleasant ○
2 USS ALGOL
3 MV STOLT DAGALI

UNITED STATES

OF AMERICA

N

North Carolina

Hatteras Inlet
Cape
Hatteras

Beaufort ○
4 SS PROTEUS
5 U-352
GRAVEYARD OF THE ATLANTIC

ATLANTIC

OCEAN

Bermuda

Florida

THE
BAHAMAS

Miami ○
Molasses Reef
Florida Keys
6 USCG BIBB
7 USCG DUANE
8 USS SPIEGEL GROVE

KEY
—·—·— International boundary
— — — State boundary
——— River
Wrecks:
Merchant ship wreck
War ship wreck
Submarine wreck

0   400 km

0   200 miles

SS ANDREA DORIA ❶

Named after a famous Italian admiral, the 29,083 ton luxury liner SS *Andrea Doria* was built by Ansaldo Societá per Azioni. Her keel was laid in their Sestri Ponente shipyards at Genoa on 9 February 1950. She was launched on 16 June 1951 by Signora Giuseppina Saragat, wife of the former Minister of the Merchant Marine, as the flagship of the luxury line Italia Societá per Azioni di Navigazione. The ship's hull was blessed by His Eminence Giuseppe Cardinal Siri, Archbishop of Genoa. Amid reports of machinery problems during sea trials, the *Andrea Doria*'s maiden voyage was delayed from 14 December 1952 to 14 January 1953. The 212m (696ft) liner had a beam of 27.4m (90ft) with Parson-geared steam turbines driving two propellers that gave a top speed of 26 knots. She was capable of carrying 218 first class, 320 cabin class and 703 tourist class passengers together with 563 officers and crew on ten decks. A veritable floating art gallery with sophistication and modern decor, she even had three open-air swimming pools – one for each class.

On 17 July 1956 the *Andrea Doria* departed Genoa on her fifty-first crossing of the Atlantic. By the evening of the 25th she was cruising through the foggy approaches to Nantucket Sound. In dense fog 73km (45 miles) south of Nantucket, at 23:22, the reinforced ice-breaking bow of the Swedish-American Line's MV *Stockholm*, outward bound from New York, powered into the centre of the *Andrea Doria*'s starboard side just aft of her bridge. The collision ripped open seven of her eleven decks, the hole reaching almost down to her keel, and killed 46 of the 1,706 passengers and crew on the *Andrea Doria* and five of the *Stockholm*'s crew. The *Andrea Doria* began to list so badly that she was unable to launch her starboard lifeboats, but fortunately she took 11 hours to sink and the tragedy was near enough to New York for an efficient rescue by several vessels. The largest, the westbound French liner SS *Ile de France* turned back to assist, shuttling its ten lifeboats back and forth to the *Andrea Doria*. The Italian liner finally capsized and sank at 10:09 on 26 July. The *Stockholm* managed to limp into port.

The day after the *Andrea Doria* sank Peter Gimbel and Joseph Fox managed to dive on the wreck and then published pictures of her in *Time* magazine. Gimbel later conducted a number of salvage operations. He recovered the First Class Bank Safe in 1981, which was opened on live television in 1984. It yielded little but American silver certificates and Italian bank notes. Once she was proved diveable the *Andrea Doria* attracted many artefact seekers despite the depth and a number of deaths. The ship's bell was taken in the late 1980s, and the statue of Genoese Admiral Andrea Doria was removed from the first class lounge. Many divers penetrate the ship through the opening cut by Peter Gimbel to retrieve the ship's safe.

Today, the *Andrea Doria* lies on her starboard side slowly collapsing in 73m (240ft) of water with unpredictable ocean currents kicking up the silt to give poor visibility. The ship is draped in monofilament fishing lines and nets. The summertime water temperature is around 7°C (45°F). Most divers penetrate the ship looking for china as a trophy. Technical diving on mixed gases has made things safer, but the dangers of penetration at this depth remain. The *Andrea Doria* has exerted her attraction on Scuba-divers from the moment she sank. She is not the deepest wreck, nor the largest, but her mystique has made her the American divers' premier challenge – the Mount Everest of wreck diving.

USS ALGOL ❷

The Andromeda class attack transport (freighter), also known as a Victory Ship, USS *Algol* saw action in World War II and in the Korean and Vietnam conflicts, and served as a support unit for the 'quarantine' of Cuba during the 1962 Cuban Missile Crisis. After being mothballed at Norfolk for some 20 years, this huge vessel was transferred to the New

Jersey Artificial Reef Program. She was environmentally cleaned, her windows, doors and hatches removed, and sunk upright on 22 November 1991. She is one of a series of Navy transports named after stars: Algol is a star in the constellation Perseus, also known as the Demon star. During her career in the US Navy she earned many commendations and several nicknames, including the 'USS Alcohol', because she carried alcoholic drinks on an early trip.

The 13,910 ton USS *Algol* (AKA-54) was 140m (459ft) long and had a beam of 19m (63ft). She was laid down on 10 December 1942 at Oakland, California, by the Moore Dry Dock Co., under a Maritime Commission contract, as SS *James Barnes*. She was launched on 17 February 1943; sponsored by Mrs J.A. McKeown and renamed *Algol* on 30 August 1943. After a session in reduced commission, she was converted to an attack cargo ship and placed in full commission on 21 July 1944.

The *Algol* was eventually decommissioned on 23 July 1970 and transferred to the Maritime Administration's National Defence Reserve Fleet. Her name was removed from the Navy list on 1 January 1977.

Today the *Algol* lies in 44m (145ft) of water with the main deck at 34m (110ft). The rudder and propeller are missing and the cargo holds are filling up with silt, but she is big and intact and worth several dives. The funnel has been removed, leaving a teardrop-shaped scar with the fat end of the teardrop pointing towards the bow. The current on the wreck can vary from slight to very strong, and the wreck has become home to a good variety of marine life.

MV STOLT DAGALI ❸

A very popular if unusual wreck, the 43m (140ft) long stern section of the MV *Stolt Dagali* is picturesque for underwater photographers. A 19,150 ton parcel tanker, 178m (583ft) long with a beam of 21m (70ft), the *Stolt Dagali* was built in 1955 by Burmeister & Wain of Copenhagen, Denmark,

and operated by Stolt-Nielsen Chartering of Norway for Pascal Tankers. Parcel tankers can carry a succession of different chemicals, edible oils, acids and other liquids in easily cleaned compartments designed to carry shipments of various sizes, temperatures and other specifications, without contamination problems.

On 26 November 1964 the *Stolt Dagali* was en route from Philadelphia to Newark, New Jersey, with a cargo of molasses, vegetable oil and solvents. At 02:00 hours she encountered dense fog as she cruised north along the New Jersey coast. The Israeli luxury liner *Shalom* was cruising south from New York harbour to the Caribbean when she collided with the *Stolt Dagali* on her port side, just behind the bridge, and cut her in two. The heavy stern section sank within minutes while the front section, buoyed by the liquids it was carrying, remained afloat. The collision pitched many crew of the *Stolt Dagali* into the cold sea, claiming the lives of 19 people. The forward two-thirds of the vessel remained afloat. It was towed to Staten Island and then Sweden, where it was fitted with a new stern and renamed.

Today, the stern section of the *Stolt Dagali* lies on its starboard side in 40m (130ft) of water and rises to within 20m (65ft) of the surface. The propeller is half buried in the sand, while the broken-off rudder is nearby. Washed by the warm waters of the Gulf Stream, she generally has excellent visibility and healthy marine life including larger pelagic species such as Mola mola and Leatherback turtles. Penetration is possible, but be careful of the depth and watch out for fishing nets.

THE GRAVEYARD OF THE ATLANTIC

Off the coast of North Carolina, aptly named the Graveyard of the Atlantic after the hundreds of ships that have sunk there, over 100 wrecks are on the regular itineraries of diving charter vessels. Located in the Gulf Stream, the diving conditions here are often easier than those found further north and in the

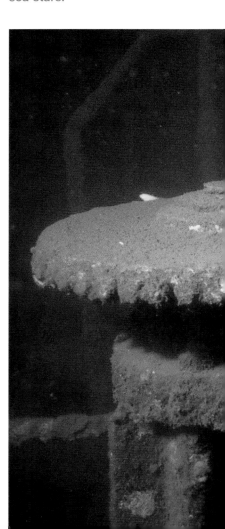

Below: The USS *Algol* – AKA-54/LKA-54 – has become home to many reef creatures such as sea stars.

late summer months the water temperatures are warm enough to find tropical species such as angelfish and butterflyfish.

SS PROTEUS ❹

One of the most popular wrecks in the area is the *Proteus*, a 4,836 ton, 124m (406ft) steamship with a beam of 14.6m (48ft), sunk after a collision with the SS *Cushing*, 40km (25 miles) south of Hatteras Inlet on 19 August 1918. Today she lies in 38m (125ft) of water with the stern mostly intact, listing to port and rising 9m (30ft) from the bottom. The wreck is mostly intact so it is easy to find one's way around. The steering mechanism is unbroken, and there are three main boilers, the propeller and another spare propeller. When first discovered, the *Proteus* had many brass artefacts but these are now rare. The animal life includes large stingrays and Cobia. Large shoals of spotted raggedtooth (sandtiger or grey nurse) sharks gather on both the stern and bow in October/November. The current ranges from slight to very strong, and the visibility is mostly greater than 18m (59ft).

U-352 ❺

Southwest of the *Proteus*, south of *Beaufort*, the U-352 was a 1,070 ton type VII-C German submarine sunk by depth charges from the United States Coastguard Cutter *Icarus* on 9 May 1942. She was 67m (220ft) long, with a beam of 6m (20ft) and powered by two diesel engines on the surface and two electric motors when submerged. Because she is a U-boat, and photogenic at that, she can get crowded. Today she lies in 35m (115ft) of water with a heavy 45 degree list to starboard. She is a relatively small wreck that can be circumnavigated twice on one dive. Most of her outer casing has corroded away, exposing the pressure hull. Animal life is good, visibility is generally better than 15m (49ft) and the currents are slight. But be careful – several divers have died on this wreck.

FLORIDA

The clear, warm waters off the Florida Keys combine reefs in marine sanctuaries and wrecks that attract novice divers and experienced deepwater wreck divers alike. The United States Coastguard Cutters *Bibb* and *Duane* were stripped of armament, their hatches were removed, parts of them were sealed against penetration, and everything was environmentally cleaned before they were sunk as artificial reefs just south of Molasses Reef in November 1987. Unfortunately, some divers have damaged or removed the barriers, allowing creatures such as turtles, as well as inexperienced divers to penetrate areas where they may become trapped.

The huge Landing Ship Dock USS *Spiegel Grove* joined the *Bibb* and *Duane* some years later.

USCG BIBB ❻

The 2,658 ton, 100m (327ft) US Treasury Class Coastguard Cutter *Bibb*'s keel was laid on 15 August 1935 and she was launched on 14 January 1937. She had a 12.5m (41ft) beam and was powered by two

Westinghouse Steam Turbines developing a total of 6,200 horsepower giving her a top speed of nearly 20 knots. She was named after the Secretary of the Treasury, George M. Bibb.

The *Bibb* served in the North Atlantic during most of World War II. She was transferred to the Pacific in 1945 and later helped in the Vietnam conflict.

She was towed to Molasses Reef, her hatches opened and her holds pumped full of water on 27 November 1987. Stripped of her armament and with her hatches and main mast removed, the *Bibb* overturned while sinking and now lies on her starboard side. Her bow faces north in 40m (131ft) of water. You will reach the port gunwale railings in only 29m (95ft) of water. Although she is a sister ship to the USCG *Duane*, they are completely different dives. With the clear waters of the Gulf Stream washing over the site, visibility can be over 30m (100ft), but a strong current is usually present. Because of the depth and being more technically challenging, the *Bibb* is less frequently visited by divers, but is popular with technical divers and in better condition than the *Duane*. The hull is encrusted with corals and harbours Goliath Groupers, Cobia, barracuda, amberjacks and turtles.

USCG DUANE ❼

The 2,658 ton, 100m (327ft) US Coastguard Treasury Class Cutter *Duane* was built at the Philadelphia Navy Yard, Philadelphia, Pennsylvania. She had a 12.5m (41ft) beam. Her keel was laid on 1 May 1935, and she was launched a year later on 3 June 1936. Named after William J. Duane, Secretary of the Treasury under Andrew Jackson, the *Duane* was commissioned on 1 August 1936.

When she was decommissioned on 1 August 1985, she was the oldest active US military vessel. The *Duane* was donated to the Keys Association of Dive Operators, stripped and environmentally prepared as an artificial reef. The doors were

removed above the main deck and the lower compartments were sealed. On 27 November 1987 she was towed to Molasses Reef: her hatches were opened, her holds were pumped full of water and she was scuttled by the US Army Corps of Engineers 0.8km (½ mile) south of the *Bibb*.

Today the *Duane* lies upright with a slight list to starboard on a sandy bottom in 37m (120ft) of water 1.5km (1 mile) south of Molasses Reef off Key Largo. One of the most spectacular dives in the Florida Keys, on a clear day the outline of *Duane*'s intact hull can be seen from above the surface. The mast and crow's nest protrude high above the hull at 18m (60ft) and the main deck lies at 30m (100ft). The hull is intact with the original rudders, propellers, railings and ladders. Lying in the Gulf Stream, visibility is usually good, but there are very strong currents. Penetration is only for those properly qualified and, like at the *Bibb*, there is good encrustation with marine life and plenty of fish and invertebrates including barracuda, angelfish, butterflyfish, jacks, grunts, snappers, wrasse and turtles.

USS SPIEGEL GROVE ❽

The 6,880 ton, 155.45m (510ft) Landing Ship Dock USS *Spiegel Grove* (LSD-32) was named after the Fremont, Ohio, estate of US President Rutherford B. Hayes, the nineteenth President of America. She had a beam of 25.6m (84ft) and was laid down by the Ingalls Shipbuilding Corp. Pascagoula, on 7 September 1954. The *Spiegel Grove* was launched on 10 November 1955, sponsored by Mrs Webb C. Hayes, and commissioned on 8 June 1956. The steam turbine-powered *Spiegel Grove* was designed to transport amphibious craft that carried combat troops ashore. A system of internal tanks could be flooded to allow up to 5m (17ft) of water to flood the well deck to create a sea-going dock. The entire stern could be opened or closed hydraulically to allow amphibious craft to drive on or off. A large part of the well deck was spanned by a helicopter deck that

could also be used as storage space for vehicles. High-capacity cranes could also be used to load or offload vehicles.

After a distinguished career the *Spiegel Grove* was decommissioned in 1989. She spent 12 years mothballed in Virginia's James River before being taken over in May 2001. She was environmentally cleaned and made safe for divers by welding doors open or shut and cutting holes in the bulkheads with the aim of scuttling her to become the third vessel in the artificial reef programme off the coast of Key Largo, Florida.

However, her scuttling, originally planned for 17 May 2002 at approximately 14:00, did not go according to plan. She began to sink prematurely, rolled over and remained upside down for several days with her bow protruding above the surface.

A salvage team managed to fully sink the vessel three weeks later, but she came to rest on her starboard side. Attempts on 10 June 2002 to right the ship using tugs and cables failed. The biggest surprise was that nature corrected the problem three years later, when currents from the waves generated by Hurricane Dennis on 9 July 2005 rocked the vessel into the upright position.

The *Spiegel Grove* now lies in 40m (130ft) of water with main deck in 24–30m (80–100ft) of water. The anti-aircraft guns and the twin propellers make excellent photographic opportunities and the hull is now coated with red algae. Though not yet covered in as much marine life as the *Bibb* and *Duane* she is quickly becoming an entire reef ecosystem. A huge vessel requiring several dives to explore, the *Spiegel Grove* is a dive not to be missed.

Above: At the time of her sinking the USS *Spiegel Grove* was the largest vessel ever sunk for divers.

BERMUDA

By Jack Jackson

Affected by the Gulf Stream, Bermuda has the northernmost coral reef system in the world. However, its treacherous reefs have over 350 registered wrecks. Often dubbed the Shipwreck Capital of the Atlantic, treasure hunters have found several wrecks in Bermuda with cargoes that included gold and jewellery. This earned it the name of Bermuda's Golden Circle.

Opposite: Part of the engine in the engine room of the *Hermes*.

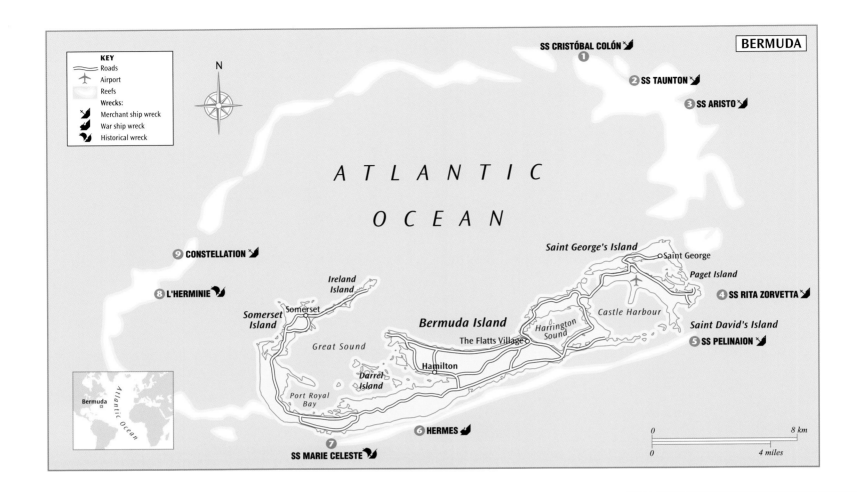

SS CRISTÓBAL COLÓN ❶

One of the largest wrecks in Bermudian waters, the 150m (492ft) Spanish luxury liner SS *Cristóbal Colón* was launched in 1923. She was heading for Mexico to load arms for the Spanish Civil War when she ran aground north of Bermuda on 25 October 1936. She was easily looted and salvaged, and during World War II US Navy aircraft pilots used her for bombing practice. Broken in two and divided by the reef, the *Cristóbal Colón*'s wreckage stretches over a large area, ranging in depth from 5m (16ft) at the bow to 25m (82ft) at the semi-intact stern. This is a huge wreck that takes several dives to cover. Like most of Bermuda's wrecks, she is relatively shallow and the marine life is prolific. Propellers, turbines, boilers

and unexploded artillery shells litter the ocean floor. The *Cristóbal Colón* remained on the reef for some time. Furniture, art and other valuables were salvaged. A year later the captain of the Norwegian steamer *Aristo* mistook the stationary *Cristóbal Colón* for a ship under way and also struck the reefs. Following this tragedy the Bermudian government dismantled the *Cristóbal Colón*'s mast and funnel to prevent other ships from making the same mistake.

SS TAUNTON ❷

A favourite shallow dive and quite photogenic, the SS *Taunton* was a 68m (223ft) Norwegian freighter built in 1902. She sank in fog on 24 November 1920. Her bow comes to within 3m (10ft) of the surface and the rest goes down to 12m (39ft) with the boilers and engines still visible. The ship's bell is on display at the Gibb's Hill Lighthouse Museum.

SS ARISTO (IRISTO) ❸

The *Aristo* was a 75m (246ft) Norwegian freighter. In 1937 her captain mistook the wreck of the *Cristóbal Colón* for a ship under way, altered course to follow her and the *Aristo* ran aground. She was towed off the reef, but soon sank and now sits bow and stern

intact with her engine, boilers and propeller still visible down to 15m (49ft). The remains of a fire engine can be found if you look closely.

SS RITA ZORVETTA ❹

The 122m (399ft) Italian freighter *Rita Zorvetta*, with a 16m (52½ft) beam, was built in Glasgow in 1919 by Stephen & Sons Ltd. She was originally named *War Gascon* and alternative spellings seen of her final name are Rita Sovetta or Rita Sorvetta. She went

Below: The *Cristóbal Colón* is one of the largest known shipwrecks in Bermudian waters. As a result of bombing practice she is spread over a large area.

aground during heavy weather off St David's Island on 13 February 1924, when the captain misread the pilot vessel's lights. No lives were lost and all the cargo was salvaged. She now lies very broken up in 6–21m (20–69ft) of water just off St David's Head with her stern relatively intact. Divers can penetrate to the boilers.

SS PELINAION ❺

One of the most popular diving sites in Bermuda, the 117m (385ft) freighter SS *Pelinaion*, with a 15m (50ft) beam, was built in Glasgow in 1907 for Hill SS Company and named Hill Glen. Her ownership changed many times before she was purchased by a Greek shipping company and given her final name in 1939. The *Pelinaion* was heading from West Africa to Baltimore when, unaware that the St David's lighthouse was blacked out due to the war, she ran aground near St David's Head on 16 January 1940. The wreck now lies in 6–21m (20–69ft) and most noticeable is the size of her boilers and engine.

HERMES ❻

The 825 ton, 50m (165ft) US Coast Guard vessel *Hermes* was built in Pennsylvania in 1943. After the war she was sold to a Filipino company and was en route to the Cape Verde Islands when she had engine trouble near Bermuda and was abandoned by her crew. She was eventually seized by the Bermudian government, cleaned up, had her hatches removed and was sunk by local dive operators as an artificial reef in 1985. She now lies nearly upright, almost intact, penetrable and with prolific marine life in 25m (82ft) of water with her mast at around 9m (30ft).

SS MARIE CELESTE ❼
(MARY CELESTIA)

The 207 ton, 69m (225ft) *Marie Celeste* was a side-wheeled paddle-steamer used as a Confederate blockade runner during the American Civil War, smuggling weapons, ammunition and supplies to the South in return for cotton and cash. Cruising at speed under a Bermudian pilot, she hit the reef on 26 September 1864. She sank in 11 minutes when towed off the reef. The ship's cook died in the sinking. Today her remains lie in 17m (56ft) of water, with one of her paddle wheel frames standing upright. The other paddle wheel lies flat on the sand along with other large sections of the ship.

L'HERMINIE ❽

The 60 gun 90m (295ft) French frigate *L'Herminie*, a three-masted, wooden hulled sailing vessel, was returning to France from Havana, Cuba, when she was wrecked on 3 December 1838. The wreck itself is in 9m (30ft) of water and has mostly rotted, leaving only the metal artefacts, but there are still 59 cannons. Divers new to the wreck would benefit from a local guide, as the site is spread over a wide area, with plenty more to see, including a huge anchor, flints for muskets and lots of musket balls.

CONSTELLATION ❾

One of the most dived wrecks in Bermuda, this 59m (192ft) four-masted, wooden hulled schooner was built in 1918. In 1932 she was sold to Robert L. Royall, refitted and renamed *Constellation*. During World War II, all available ships were pressed into the Merchant Navy and the *Constellation* sailed from New York for La Guira, Venezuela, but she started to leak. Headed to Bermuda for repairs she struck either the reef or the wreck of the *Montana* and was lost on 31 July 1943. All of the crew of the vessel survived.

Today the *Constellation* lies in 9m (30ft) of water, exposing sacks of petrified cement, which rise to within 2.5m (8ft) of the surface. The wreck is often referred to as the Dime Store or Woolworths Wreck because of the assortment of small items to be seen. Together with the *Montana*, she formed the basis for Peter Benchley's book, and the subsequent 1977 film, *The Deep*.

Opposite: The *Marie Celeste* is mostly covered in sand, but her paddle wheels are a major attraction for divers and marine life alike.

BAHAMAS AND CARIBBEAN

By Lawson Wood and Jack Jackson (introduction and Dutch Antilles)

An arm of the Atlantic, the Caribbean has delightful islands, warm waters, a mild tropical climate, a potpourri of diverse cultures and a laid-back attitude to life. The islands and connecting ridges of the eastern Caribbean prevent the interchange of deep water from the eastern Atlantic, reducing tides and increasing visibility. Most Caribbean diving is relatively free of strong currents. The Atlantic was cut off from the Pacific before some species could reach it so there is less diversity of marine life than in the Indo-Pacific; there are no clownfish or brightly coloured soft tree corals. Destinations where diving is important to the economy have marine reserves and wrecks with fixed mooring buoys, and several destinations have themed animal encounters as well as coral reefs and plenty of wrecks.

Opposite: Theo's Wreck off Grand Bahama Island lies at 90 degrees to the vertical on her port side and is a very popular wreck dive.

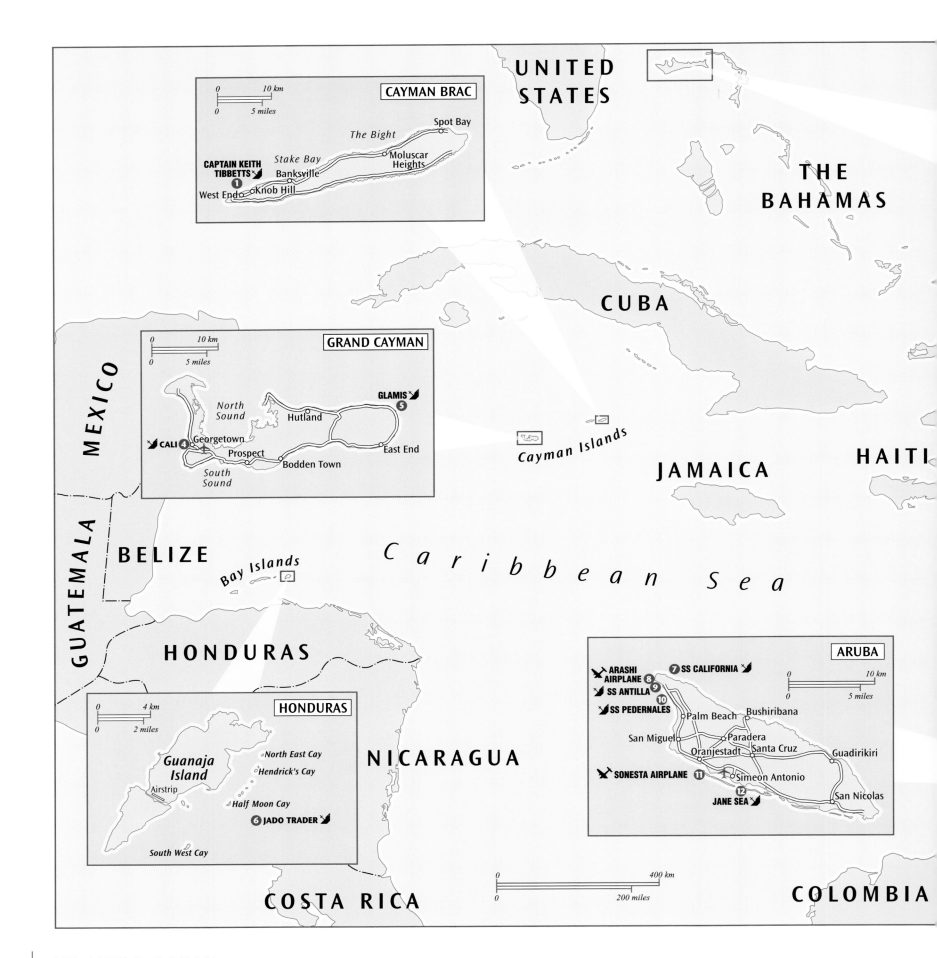

CAYMAN BRAC

0 ——— 10 km
0 ——— 5 miles

Spot Bay
The Bight
Stake Bay   Moluscar Heights
CAPTAIN KEITH TIBBETTS
Banksville
West End   Knob Hill

GRAND CAYMAN

0 ——— 10 km
0 ——— 5 miles

North Sound
GLAMIS
Hutland
CALI   Georgetown
Prospect   East End
Bodden Town
South Sound

UNITED STATES

THE BAHAMAS

CUBA

Cayman Islands

JAMAICA

HAITI

MEXICO

GUATEMALA

BELIZE

Bay Islands

Caribbean Sea

HONDURAS

HONDURAS

0 ——— 4 km
0 ——— 2 miles

Guanaja Island
North East Cay
Hendrick's Cay
Airstrip
Half Moon Cay
JADO TRADER
South West Cay

NICARAGUA

ARUBA

0 ——— 10 km
0 ——— 5 miles

ARASHI AIRPLANE   SS CALIFORNIA
SS ANTILLA
SS PEDERNALES   Palm Beach   Bushiribana
San Miguel   Paradera   Santa Cruz
Oranjestad   Guadirikiri
SONESTA AIRPLANE   Simeon Antonio
JANE SEA   San Nicolas

COSTA RICA

400 km
200 miles

COLOMBIA

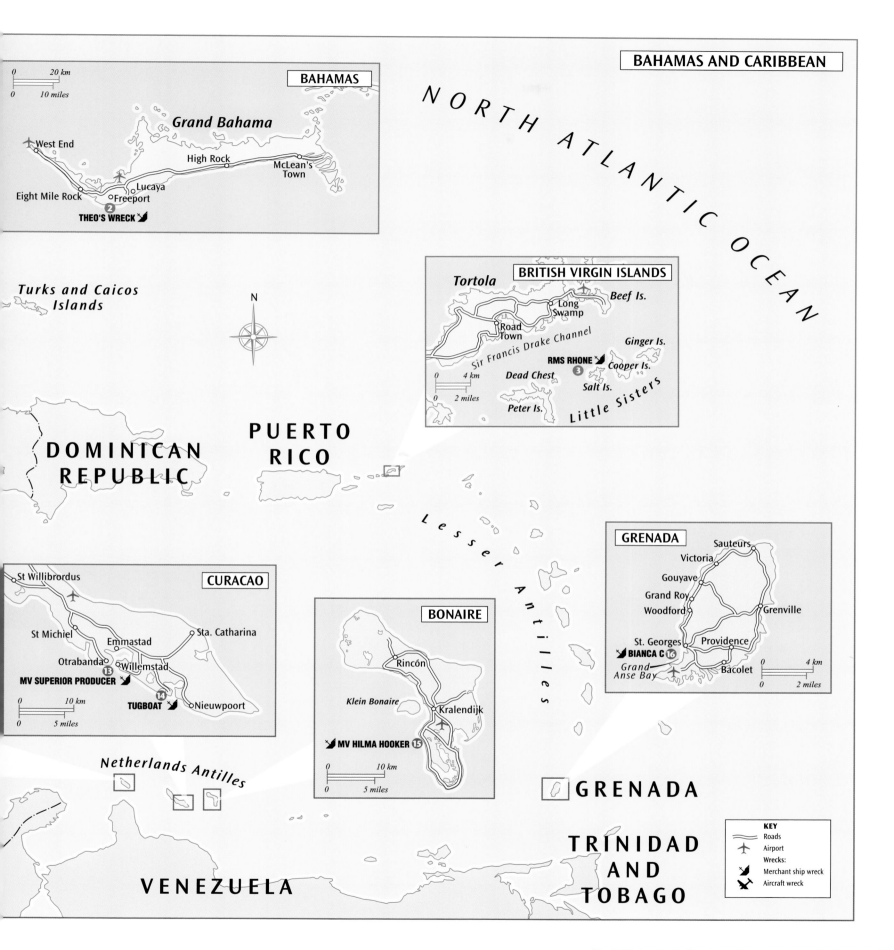

BAHAMAS

0 20 km
0 10 miles

Grand Bahama

West End

High Rock

McLean's
Town

Eight Mile Rock

Lucaya
Freeport

② THEO'S WRECK

*Turks and Caicos
Islands*

N

BRITISH VIRGIN ISLANDS

Tortola

Beef Is.

Long
Swamp

Road
Town

Sir Francis Drake Channel

Ginger Is.

RMS RHONE
③

Cooper Is.

Dead Chest

0 4 km

0 2 miles

Salt Is.

Peter Is.

Little Sisters

NORTH ATLANTIC OCEAN

**PUERTO
RICO**

**DOMINICAN
REPUBLIC**

Lesser Antilles

GRENADA

Sauteurs

Victoria

Gouyave

Grand Roy

Woodford

Grenville

St. Georges

BIANCA C ⑯

*Grand
Anse Bay*

Providence

Bacolet

0 4 km

0 2 miles

CURACAO

St Willibrordus

St Michiel

Emmastad

Sta. Catharina

Otrabanda

Willemstad

⑬
MV SUPERIOR PRODUCER

⑭
TUGBOAT

Nieuwpoort

0 10 km

0 5 miles

BONAIRE

Rincón

Klein Bonaire

Kralendijk

MV HILMA HOOKER ⑮

0 10 km

0 5 miles

Netherlands Antilles

G R E N A D A

**T R I N I D A D
A N D
T O B A G O**

V E N E Z U E L A

KEY
Roads
Airport
Wrecks:
Merchant ship wreck
Aircraft wreck

With majestic reefs, rich walls, shoals of colourful fish, large pelagics, invertebrates, gorgonias, colour from myriad of sponges, wrecks, caverns and breathtaking visibility, whether you are a novice or a super-fit seasoned veteran the Caribbean guarantees excellent diving. Although the islands vary from mountainous and tropical to almost flat and arid, the diving does not vary that much. The islands bordering the Atlantic Ocean have more of the larger pelagic species on their Atlantic coasts. Much stronger currents give exciting drift-dives off such places as Cozumel and Tobago, and the trade winds produce rough seas that are usually only divided on the rare occasions when the wind direction veers on islands' windward sides, for instance with Aruba, Bonaire and Curaçao.

Most of the islands are fringed by coral reefs and have gentle currents. Add sophisticated infrastructures, a mild tropical climate, ideal conditions for novices and leisurely diving, a potpourri of diverse cultures and a laid-back attitude to life, and one gets perfect destinations for divers on vacation. The Bahamas and Caribbean are particularly popular with those who only dive a few times a year or have non-diving companions.

BAHAMAS

THEO'S WRECK ❷

Grand Bahama has a very mixed terrain with an ancient limestone rocky base and small rolling hills covered in scrubby vegetation. As you fly over the island, you are struck by the colour of the water, ranging from light turquoise through blue, to the near-black of the circular sink holes inland, to the green of the shallow grass beds, dropping off to indigo blue off the wall, where the majority of the diving is undertaken. The dive centres on Grand Bahama all operate along the same stretch of southern coastline, and all the sites have mooring buoys to prevent anchor damage.

The reefs along the south shore of Grand Bahama Island are of a classic 'spur and groove' formation which indicates that they have been formed by wind and wave action over millennia, with the 'spurs' constructed of good-quality corals and the 'grooves' being formed by surf and wave surge during periodic winter storms. There is a secondary inner barrier reef, very similar to the reef formations around Bermuda. This protects the islands from the worst of the storms.

Theo's Wreck is located almost due south from Freeport and was built as the MS *Logna* in Norway in 1954. She was later sold and renamed the MV *Island Cement*. She was named Theo's Wreck after Theodopolis Galanoupoulos, an engineer who worked with the Bahama Cement Company. It was his idea to sink the ship as an artificial reef at the end of her useful career. With the help of The Underwater Exploration Soceity (UNEXSO), Theo's Wreck was finally sunk off the Silver Beach Inlet on 16 October 1982. The ship now rests on her port side, with her stern hanging over the edge of the drop-off.

The underside of the hull, including the propeller and rudder, is smothered in Orange Cup Corals (*Tubastrea coccinea*), and almost the entire superstructure is covered in colourful sponges. There are numerous safe entry points to gain access to the bridge and engine rooms. A large, friendly, Green Moray Eel inhabits this area. Being so close to the edge of the drop-off almost guarantees large schools of snapper, grunt and jacks. You will also find all the regular exotic tropical Caribbean fish species such as angelfish and butterflyfish. Tarpon, huge Rainbow Parrotfish and turtles are also found around the wreck.

While this is regarded as a deep dive, you must try and dive the wreck at night as well as during the day. It comes alive at night when the colourful sponges and corals are illuminated by divers' torches. Theo's Wreck is regarded as a special area of conservation by the Bahamas National Trust.

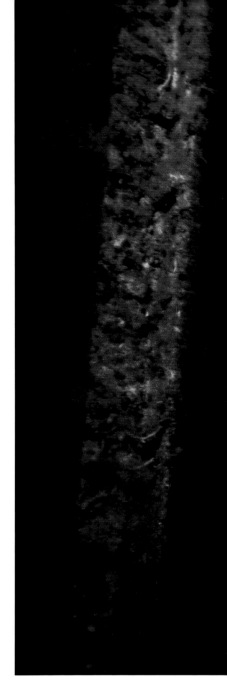

Above: The interior of Theo's Wreck is accessible to divers, who can explore her empty cargo holds.

BRITISH VIRGIN ISLANDS

RMS RHONE ❸

Built by Millwall Iron Works for The Royal Mail
Steam Packet Company and launched on
11 February 1865, the 2,738 ton Royal Mail Steamer
Rhone had a length of 97m (317ft) and a beam of
12m (40ft). She had berths for 253 first class
passengers, 30 second class and 30 third class.
Regarded as one of the finest ships of the time, her
seafaring capabilities were demonstrated when she

survived the hurricane conditions that sank her
sistership RMS *London* in 1866.

During the 1860s, Tortola, in the British Virgin
Islands, was still a sleepy backwater and it was her
neighbour, Charlotte Amalie on St Thomas Island
in the United States Virgin Islands, that developed
as a bustling port. When yellow fever broke out in St
Thomas, the transatlantic steamers avoided the
island. They transferred their operations to Road
Harbour on Tortola and Great Harbour on Peter
Island to refuel and transfer passengers and goods.

The *Rhone*, under the command of Captain Robert F. Wooley, was at anchor outside Great Harbour on Peter Island on the morning of 29 October 1867, and was in the process of taking on stores for the return journey when the first indications of a gathering storm were felt. Fortunately the majority of the *Rhone*'s passengers had disembarked and she only had 18 passengers, plus the crew of 129, aboard when the storm struck suddenly and violently. Captain Wooley attempted to take the *Rhone* out to sea to ride out the storm, but her anchor chain caught and snapped and she suddenly dropped her 1,300kg (3,000lb) anchor. At that moment the wind changed direction to the southeast, struck the ship and she foundered on Salt Island. So sudden was this assault that the hull split open on the shallow reef and the ship sank immediately, taking with her all but one passenger and twenty-one of the crew. The survivors were picked up the next day, some having climbed the mast to safety, others having clung to bits of the ship that had come free when the *Rhone* sank. There is a

Above: Divers can easily swim through the remains of the RMS *Rhone*.

mass grave on Salt Island. The wreck of the RMS *Rhone* is well known for its starring role in the film version of Peter Benchley's novel *The Deep* and now lies in two distinct parts from 6–27m (20–89ft).

The forward part of the hull and bowsprit are lying to starboard and are in the deepest water. The hull is completely open, and you are able to swim through the ribs of the ship, where there are numerous schools of snapper and squirrelfish. The shaded areas of the ship's hull are completely covered in Orange Cup Corals and small colourful hydroids. Encrusting corals, small sea fans and plumes adorn the upturned port side of the hull. All the wooden decking has now rotted away, allowing easy access throughout the ship. The foremast and crow's nest are still fairly intact, now lying partly on the seabed. Aft of this fore section of the wreck the boiler and part of the mid-section of the wreck can be found, where a large section of ribs makes for a great photograph.

The stern of the ship, still with its four-bladed bronze propeller embedded in the reef, is now completely opened up. You can swim along the entire length of the propeller shaft to the gearbox, which is now home to squirrel fish, snapper, Banded Coral Shrimps and various encrusting and brightly coloured corals. Under the stern, next to the rudder, there are generally small schools of snapper. A further two large sections of rib stand upright, making an interesting backdrop to your photographs.

The wreck of the *Rhone* is one of the best dives in the Caribbean, and even though it is heavily dived, it is amazing just how much marine life is present on and around the wreck. The addition of mooring buoys has prevented anchor damage, and the area is a protected Marine National Park. The dive guides and instructors who are part of the British Virgin Islands Diving Operators Association all give a very thorough brief on each part of the dive, paying particular attention to your buoyancy and the need to keep off the corals.

CAYMAN ISLANDS

The Cayman Islands have always been synonymous with crystal-clear waters, an abundance of marine life and fabulous vertical walls covered in corals. Indeed, the Cayman Islands always appear in diver polls of the top ten diving locations in the world. However, not too many people are aware of the maritime heritage of the Cayman Islands and the number of shipwrecks around the shores. There are over 150 shipwrecks, dating back over five centuries, since Christopher Columbus first sighted the islands. Travelling with his last two remaining caravels *La Capitana* and *Santiago de Palos*, Columbus's fleet was blown off course while trying to reach the safety of Santo Domingo (Dominican Republic) to repair his badly leaking craft. Passing by Little Cayman and Cayman Brac in May 1503, they first thought them no more than navigational hazards and made their way on to Cuba. It is this legacy that we now explore, with the greatest number of shipwrecks being found off the East End of Grand Cayman.

The reason why so many ships visited Cayman waters is twofold. Firstly, ships visited the islands to stock up with turtles, fish and fresh water. Turtles were an essential part of the live and cured (salted) food stores that all merchant ships required to help stave off scurvy. Secondly, the island of 'Caiman Grande' was one of the most important islands for navigation, as the East End reefs marked the passage northwest to Cuba and thence into the Gulf Stream to the route back across the Atlantic Ocean to Europe.

The legacy of the Cayman Islands is the sea itself, her people and her rich and abundant waters. Now, 500 years after the discovery of the islands, the Cayman shipwrecks are delighting the diving world. Some of the shipwrecks have been intentionally placed as artificial reefs and diver interest sites, while others have ended up on the shallow coral reefs by accident. Some shipwrecks in Cayman waters can be dived from shore, such as the *Barbara Ann*, *Cali*, *David Nicholson*, *Kissimmee*, *Prince Frederick* and the *Topsy*; the *Kirk Pride* can be seen from a submersible; and dive boats go out to the *Balboa*, *Captain Keith Tibbetts*, *Cayman Mariner*, *Doc Poulson*, *Glamis*, *Oro Verde*, *Pallas*, *Ridgefield* and many more. For technical divers there are weekly trips to the deep *Carrie Lee* wreck and, when weather permits, the *12 Mile Bank Fuel Barge* is a rare treat!

Night diving, deep diving, day trips, photography, marine biology and more can be done on these wrecks. Ships, whether sunk intentionally or by accident, offer a unique attraction that everyone wants to see. The shipwrecks also offer a chance for the natural reefs in close proximity to have some relief through colonization on the wrecks. Artificial reefs do not replace the existing natural habitats, but rather augment the existing reefs and soon become encrusted with all manner of marine life.

Below: Sunk deliberately in 1996, MV *Captain Keith Tibbetts*, a former Russian frigate, is gradually opening up as it deteriorates, and is now covered in a patina of colourful corals, sponges and invertebrates.

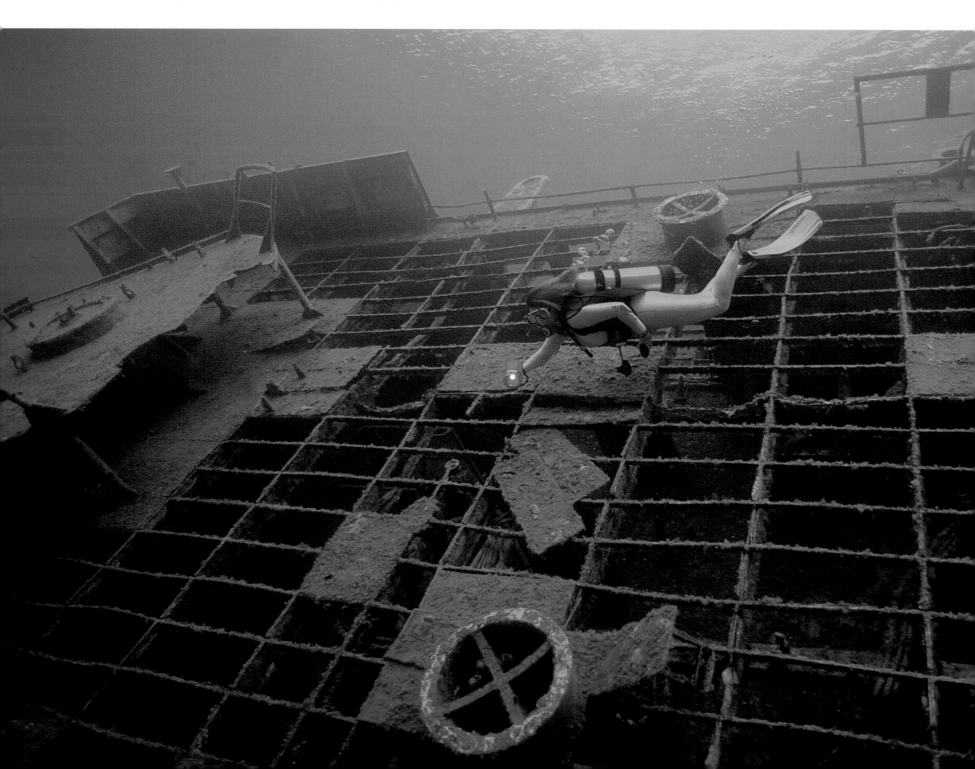

A SMALL SELECTION OF THE BEST ON OFFER

CAYMAN BRAC

MV CAPTAIN KEITH TIBBETTS ❶

The 1,590 ton Russian Frigate, Patrol Vessel No. 356, was a Brigadier Type II Class Frigate built in 1984 at Nakhodka in the USSR at a cost of US$30 million. The ship is 101m (330ft) long with a beam of 13m (42½ft). Originally part of the old Soviet fleet stationed in Cuba during the Cold War, the vessel was never involved in any conflict. When the USSR dissolved in 1992, the newly created Russian Republic took over the operational control of the Soviet base on Cuba. Unfortunately, due to the economic upheaval in Russia, the base could not be supported financially, and in 1993 the base and all the ships stationed in the Caribbean were removed from active duty. Patrol Vessel No. 356 was bought by the Cayman government and renamed MV *Captain Keith Tibbetts* after a well-known and honoured Brac statesman. It was sunk deliberately in September 1996, making a welcome addition to Cayman wreck diving.

Underwater, the ship is simply massive and since 1996 it has been transformed. The fore section has been virtually ripped off and now lies almost on its port side at around 75 degrees to the vertical. The turbines and other engine parts lie exposed in the broken area amidships, while the aft section, listing slightly to port, gives easy access into the interior. All the metal surfaces are covered in a patina of sponges, corals, hydroids and algae. Large groupers, barracuda and eels have made their homes on the wreck, and the variety of marine life on show at night is simply staggering. On either side of the wreck are healthy sections of coral reef carpeted with huge barrel sponges. Under the bow at 25m (82ft) is a field of Garden Eels.

GRAND CAYMAN

GLAMIS ❺

On a small section of reef near the East End channel of Grand Cayman is a shallow wreck that is an impressive diving and snorkelling site. Research by the National Maritime Museum in London and the Sjøfartsmuseum at Bygdøynes in Oslo, Norway, has now confirmed that these are the remains of the *Glamis*.

Lloyd's Register and Lloyd's List tell us that the *Glamis* was one of 21 ships built by Stephen & Sons of the Dundee Shipbuilders Company in 1876. She was a 1,232 ton, 69m (225¼ft) three-masted iron and steel barque. The *Glamis* was sold to L. Lydersen of Norway in 1905, who kept her for six years before N.A. Lydersen became the owner in 1911. Travelling from Savannah, Georgia, to Muhlgraben, with a cargo of logwood, she was under the helm of Master Thomas Tørbjørnsen when she was forced onto the reefs at East End, Grand Cayman on 14 August 1913. Stuck fast on the jagged elkhorn coral barrier reef, she had to be condemned.

Today the ship's hull is split open and folded outwards. One of her huge anchors sits almost upright on the coral platform, the stem and flukes supported by the iron stock. To the north of the open hull are the windlass, anchor winch, capstan, rudder assembly, deck hatches, bollards and items of rigging. This shallow wreck is also perfect for snorkelling over and is shallow enough for easy exploration. Large numbers of snappers and grunts can be found all around the wreck and as you go off the stern to the northeast; the flat coral platform evolves into the classic spur and groove reef associated with the Cayman Islands. To the south of the wreck is at least one, but possibly two other ships, much older than the *Glamis*, and of wooden construction (as no hull remains can be found). Their anchors and chain are of a different design and age.

CALI ❹

The 1,080 ton *Cali* was built in Dumbarton, Scotland, by A. MacMillan & Sons Ltd., and originally launched as the *Hawaii* in 1900. Built for Hind, Rolph and Company, of San Francisco, she was a 63m (206ft) four-masted barquentine. She circumnavigated the world at least four times while transporting cargoes of lumber, coal, coffee and rice. She once became trapped in Antarctic ice near South Georgia in the southern Atlantic. Having made a fortune from her, the influential owners (one of whom, James Rolph Jnr, became Governor of California) sold the *Hawaii* after she had languished unused in Seattle harbour for four years.

She was sold to Captain E.R. Sterling of Seattle in May 1926, who installed two 240-horsepower diesel engines. During this conversion, she retained her masts but lost her sails and bowsprit and became a 'bald-headed four-masted schooner'. She was renamed the *Ethel M. Sterling* after Captain Sterling's daughter-in-law. The *Ethel M. Sterling* plied the trade routes until she was seized in San Francisco in September 1927, because her owners had never paid for the engines. The ship was subsequently sold to a woman in Los Angeles for use as a tender in the tuna trade. Proving too big for the job, she was sold again to the Santa Fe Mercantile Company and used for lumber movements. Sold once more to Mexican owners in 1933, she was fully converted to a powered motor ship and lost her masts.

Renamed the MV *Hidalgo*, her Mexican owners used her principally along the western Pacific coastline. When war escalated, she expanded her route into the Caribbean, travelling through the Panama Canal many times. She continued with a very illustrious career and was eventually sold to a 'Colombian Interest' in 1946 and had her name changed for the last time to the *Cali*.

On 9 January 1948, while carrying a cargo of 30,000 bags of rice from Guayaquill, Ecuador, to Santiago de Cuba, the now ageing hull developed a

serious leak during foul weather, and the *Cali* changed course and put into George Town, Grand Cayman. The leak grew more serious and the crew decided to run her ashore to save the cargo of rice. The *Cali* was finally abandoned on 27 January 1948. Known locally as the Rice Ship, the appalling smell of the remainder of the rotting rice hung like a pall over George Town for many months. There she remained, unloved and abandoned; further wrecked by vandals who set her on fire, she burned to the waterline and sank. The *Cali* was registered as a navigation hazard, and subsequently blown apart by the British military.

The *Cali* is now scattered over a wide area of the seabed, fairly flattened, but there are still many recognizable parts, including the engines, anchor winch, davits, bollards and prop-shafts. It is possible to find traces of sail, steam and six-cylinder diesel engines for handling sails and anchors. The base of the boiler contains firebricks and the winch is amidships. The engine manufacturer's name, Cooper Bessemer, is just legible on the rocker box casting.

Above: The remains of the *Cali* were blown apart and are now spread over a large area.

Two lifeboat davits are still swung over the stern. A friendly turtle inhabits the area and is seen on most dives. There is little coral cover due to the wreck's proximity to the harbour, but there is plenty of fish life, including Rainbow Parrotfish (*Scarus guacamaia*) and numerous species of groupers, snappers and grunts. Large numbers of invertebrates can be found on dives at dusk and at night. Being so close to the shore, the *Cali* is an excellent wreck dive for all levels of diver, and cruise ship tourists snorkel over the site daily. Further to the north of the wreckage can be found the ballast pile and a number of small artefacts from the former schooner *Arbatus II*.

GRENADA

BIANCA C ⓰

The *Bianca C* had a curious and somewhat chequered career during her lifespan. She was originally laid down in 1939 at Construction Navales, La Ciotat, on the Mediterranean coast near Marseille. The unfinished 180m (591ft) ship was launched in June 1944 as the *Maréchal Pétain*. She was towed to Port Bou, where the Germans sank her, in August, during their retreat from southern France. The sunken hull was subsequently renamed *La Marseillaise*, raised and towed back to her builder's shipyard at La Ciotat in 1946, where she was refitted as a cruise ship for Messageries Maritimes of Marseille. Completed in July 1949, she entered service as a world-travelling cruise liner. In 1957 she was sold to Arosa Line Inc. of Panama, who renamed her *Arosa Sky*, but they only kept her for two years before selling her to G. Costa Du Genoa in 1959, where she was refitted, had her tonnage increased and was renamed the *Bianca C*. The ship plied a regular route from Naples to Venezuela, with regular stops at Caribbean islands such as Grenada.

On 22 October 1961 the Grenada islanders woke to shrill blasts from the cruise liner. An explosion had occurred in her engine room and there was insufficient firefighting equipment on board to control the engulfing flames. The fire quickly spread throughout the ship, and many yachts and other craft in the area rushed to her aid and evacuated the passengers. The British frigate HMS *Londonderry* attempted to pull the ship into shallower water and away from the shipping lanes, but the towrope snapped and the *Bianca C* went down in 51m (167ft) of water.

The wreck is largely intact, apart from the collapsed stern section, which took the brunt of the impact of the 18,000 ton ship. Her propellers were removed for scrap in the 1970s. The ship leans heavily to starboard and is really quite spectacular to dive. The bridge and upper structures are all intact, although her hatch covers are long gone. Coral, algae and sponge growth now covers all the exposed metalwork; due to the depth it is best to bring flashlights to see the true colours on this massive shipwreck. Barracuda, kingfish, jacks and pompano can be found in the water column and the decks are surrounded by the usual snappers, grunts and other tropical fish. The bows of the ship are intact and covered in marine growth. The sheer scale of the ship justifies its nickname of Titanic of the Caribbean.

HONDURAS

JADO TRADER ❻

Weighing approximately 7,000 tons and 69m (226ft) long, the *Jado Trader* was an inter-island freighter transporting fruit and other supplies around a number of Caribbean ports. However, during a routine inspection by the Honduras police, they discovered that she was also transporting marijuana. She was confiscated, her was cargo destroyed and she lay in dock for several years, gradually deteriorating.

Eventually, a number of tour operators and diving companies managed to purchase the ship from the Honduran government, and a full environmental clean-up was carried out. The *Jado Trader* was sunk

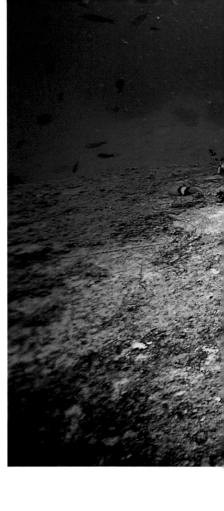

as a diver attraction, near two coral pinnacles, on a flat, sandy seabed in 1985. The ship now lies on her starboard side and is virtually intact. The entire superstructure is covered in brilliantly coloured green, red and orange sponges. Small stony corals and sea fans can also be found, but it is the sponges that set this wreck apart from others in the Caribbean. The winches are very photogenic, as is the main mast and bridge. The *Jado Trader* is known for its very large grouper, as well as friendly moray eels and angelfish.

DUTCH ANTILLES

ARUBA

Aruba is known as the wreck capital of the Caribbean, but avoid the peak cruise ship months of December and January, since the most popular sites tend to be crowded with their block-bookings.

The island is well known for the number of ships and aircraft that have been intentionally sunk for divers. Some, particularly the aircraft, have been broken up by the weather. Others, like the 74m (243ft) Colombian freighter *Star Gerren*, which was sunk in August 2000 in front of the high-rise strip by Hadicurari, have not become popular dives.

SS CALIFORNIA ❼

Southeast of the lighthouse in the Hudishibana area the SS *California* is an interesting wreck at a good depth for underwater photography. The wreck rises to 9m (30ft) and is surrounded by large coral formations and an abundance of reef fish. However, it is located in the choppy seas and strong currents of the island's windward side. This makes it often difficult to reach and only suitable for advanced divers and then only during unusually calm weather on this side of the island. The best months for this are September and October.

The SS *California* was a wooden-hulled brig or barquentine that ran aground off the Hudishibana

area on the north coast at night on 23 September 1891. The remains are scattered about, covered in sponges, cup corals and anemones, and attract large groupers. The only large objects left are an engine block and an anchor.

The nearby shoreline is now popularly called The California Dunes and the lighthouse is referred to as the California Lighthouse.

This was not the ship that failed to respond to mayday calls from the SS *Titanic* when she hit an iceberg in 1912; that vessel was the SS *Californian*. She was torpedoed by a German U-boat off Cape Matapan, Greece, on 9 November 1915 during World War I.

ARASHI AIRPLANE ❽

There used to be two airplanes off Arashi Beach, but the smaller one, a Lockheed LoneStar, has disintegrated. The twin-engined Beechcraft sits in 10m (33ft) of water. The basic aeroplane is still there, but the propellers have fallen off. The passenger cabin is full of shoaling fish. This is an easy site for beginners, with a maximum depth of 15m (49ft).

SS ANTILLA ❾

Off Malmok Beach is one of the largest wrecks and best dive sites in the Caribbean. The 4,400 ton, 122m (400ft) *Antilla* was a German freighter built in 1937 at the Finkenwarder shipyard in Hamburg. She was scuttled off Malmok Beach on 10 May 1940 by her captain in response to a demand to surrender. She was suspected of supplying a wolf pack of German U-boats during World War II and, because of her captain's ability to elude pursuers, became known in the Caribbean as the ghost ship. Aruba was Dutch territory and *Antilla* was anchored off the western shore when the Germans invaded Holland. The authorities gave the vessel's captain 24 hours to surrender, but he ordered the boilers to be supercharged and then flooded her engine compartment causing an explosion that ripped the

Left: The fuselage of Aruba's Arashi Airplane is easily penetrated.

ship in two. She now lies in 18m (59ft) of water, listing to port.

The wreck has large compartments so it is easily penetrated. Having spent more than 60 years in warm water, it is covered in tube sponges, cup corals, tunicates, hydroids, corals and fan worms. The fish life includes Sergeant Majors, parrotfish, moray eels, trumpetfish, snappers, Queen Angelfish, very large groupers and many species of shoaling fish. Shoals of Silversides are common during spring and early summer. Part of the wreck's starboard side is above water and used by seabirds. Pelicans can be seen diving during the day.

This wreck requires several dives and is popular as a night dive. There is frequently a strong current. Several diving and snorkelling boats are often moored on the wreck at the same time.

SS PEDERNALES ⑩

Lying off Hadicurari Beach is the *Pedernales*, an oil tanker torpedoed by the German submarine U-156 on 16 February 1942 during World War II. The US

military cut the wreck into three pieces. The midsection, badly damaged by the torpedo, was left behind, while the bow and stern were towed to America. These were welded together into a smaller vessel, which took part in the Allied invasion of Normandy on D-day as a landing craft.

What is left now lies in several large pieces at 8m (25ft), with the tanker's pipeline system, cabins, wash basins, lavatories, etc. spread out between coral formations. An easy dive that is delightful for its prolific fish life, it is ideal for novices though there is often a strong current and poor visibility. The maximum depth is 11m (36ft). Just west of the *Pedernales* is a DC-3 Dakota aircraft, sunk there by the Aruban Watersports Association in 9m (30 feet) of water on 8 August 1998.

SONESTA AIRPLANE ⑪

This site, off Sonesta Island, used to have two aeroplanes. However, the Beechcraft-18 has disintegrated. A Convair-400 that was confiscated by the Aruban Government for drug smuggling was sunk here and now lies in 15m (49ft) of water. The main doors and most of the interior of the aircraft were removed, so the wreck is easy to penetrate. It was broken up by the surge from Hurricane Lenny in 1999.

JANE SEA ⑫

East of Skalahein, the spectacular *Jane Sea* was a 75m (246ft) cement freighter that was sunk intentionally as an artificial reef. It is lying upright with the 2m (6½ft) propeller at 29m (95ft), the deck at 18m (59ft), the aft wheelhouse at 14m (46ft) and the bow at 15m (49ft). The cargo area is open from the top, but penetrating the rest of the wreck is only for experienced wreck divers.

There is plenty of colour: Orange Cup Corals, fire coral and red and pink encrusting sponges are found on the hull, and there are some Black Corals on the wreck's port side. The wreck attracts shoaling fish, barracuda, lobsters and Green Moray Eels, while Brain Corals and Gorgonian Sea Fans can be found around her.

The reef is parallel to the island at the south coast and the *Jane Sea* is facing the reef. In poor visibility divers can find the ship's anchor chain at the bottom of the mooring rope and follow it in an arc to the right, first up the reef, where there are good large coral heads, and then down the reef to the bow of the wreck. The superstructure and propeller are great for photography. There can be a very strong current and the maximum depth is 29m (95ft).

BONAIRE

With over 30,000 diving visitors each year Bonaire vies with Grand Cayman and Cozumel as the top Caribbean destination for American divers. The least developed and least populated of the ABC islands, Bonaire is a world leader in the preservation of underwater resources. The island is a protected marine park. Divers must attend a diver-orientation session dealing with Bonaire Marine Park regulations when purchasing the necessary Marine Park tag. Various local vessels have sunk in Bonaire's waters, including the historic 18.3m (60ft) *Our Confidence*, which sank in 17m (55ft) of water 46m (150ft) west of Harbour Village Resort on 4 August 2003.

MV HILMA HOOKER ⑮

South of The Lake, north of Angel City, is the 1,027 ton Korean freighter MV *Hilma Hooker*. She had a length of 72m (235ft) and a beam of 11m (36ft). On 12 September 1984 she was deliberately sunk by the Bonaire dive operators. Unfortunately, no one thought to remove the anti-fouling, so marine organisms have been slow to establish themselves on the hull. Built in Holland in 1951, the ship was known variously as the *Midsland*, *Mistral*, *William Express*, *Anna* and *Doric Express* before becoming the *Hilma Hooker*. She had docked at the Town Pier for urgent repairs, but alert customs officers found

Below: In common with the rest of the Caribbean, sponges are the most colourful parts on the engine of the Sonesta Airplane in Aruba.

marijuana hidden on board so the ship was confiscated and the haul burnt.

A cluster of dive buoys along the wreck now marks the site. The ship rests on her starboard side at the bottom of the reef slope with the highest point of the vessel at 18m (59ft). The structure is being colonized by sponges, and is shelter to Tiger and Black Groupers, Black Margates, Mahogany Snappers and Yellowtail Snappers. Large Horse-eye Jacks cruise the open water beyond the wreck. Except where there are large open compartments in the central section, penetration of the wreck is inadvisable, except by advanced divers. The average depth is 25m (82ft), the maximum depth is 30m (98ft) and currents can be strong.

CURAÇAO

Curaçao is much larger than either Aruba or Bonaire and is not as popular a dive destination as Bonaire,

even though it has similar reefs. The entire western side of the island, from Noordpunt (North Point) to Oostpunt (East Point), is one large dive site with three underwater parks.

MV SUPERIOR PRODUCER ⓭

Just west of the harbour entrance, Curaçao's top wreck dive, the 70m (230ft) *Superior Producer*, sits upright on sand at 34m (112ft). Her wheelhouse is at 25m (82ft) and a mast rises to 15m (50ft). Parts of the hull and the interior of the wheelhouse are coated with Orange Tubastrea Cup Corals and colourful encrusting sponges. There are larger reef fish including barracuda and groupers.

The vessel sank in September 1977 when she was outward bound from Santa Anna Bay, Willemstad, with goods bound for Columbia. Heavy seas shifted the cargo of clothes and, just outside the harbour, the ship began to take on water. Unable to be saved, she was towed away from the channel to be sunk. Several local divers required recompression treatment when they pirated the cargo. Divers snorkelling from the shore should have a surface marker buoy and watch out for boat traffic.

TUGBOAT ⓮

At the protected southeast side of Caracas Bay the tugboat is one of Curaçao's most popular dives. The tugboat, which is small enough to be photographed in its entirety, lies upright on sand at 5m (16ft) carpeted with multicoloured tube sponges and Orange Tubastrea Cup Corals. This tiny tugboat had been manoeuvring a tanker when the captain dropped the anchor onto the deck of the tugboat, causing its sinking.

To the southeast of the tugboat there is a steep drop-off beginning at about 9m (30ft), and dropping to about 30m (98ft) before shelving out at 45 degrees or less with stony corals and gorgonias. The fish are used to being hand-fed. The average depth is 5m (16ft) and the maximum depth is 40m (131ft).

GREAT BRITAIN AND REP. OF IRELAND

By Jack Jackson and Lawson Wood (Scotland)

Divers are spoilt for choice when it comes to wrecks in these waters, although conditions are rarely ideal and currents and depth can cause problems. Winter storms, a treacherous coastline and two world wars in the 20th century have left countless wrecks to be enjoyed when the weather allows.

Opposite: A diver penetrating the USS Liberty Ship *James Eagan Layne*, one of the most popular wrecks in the UK.

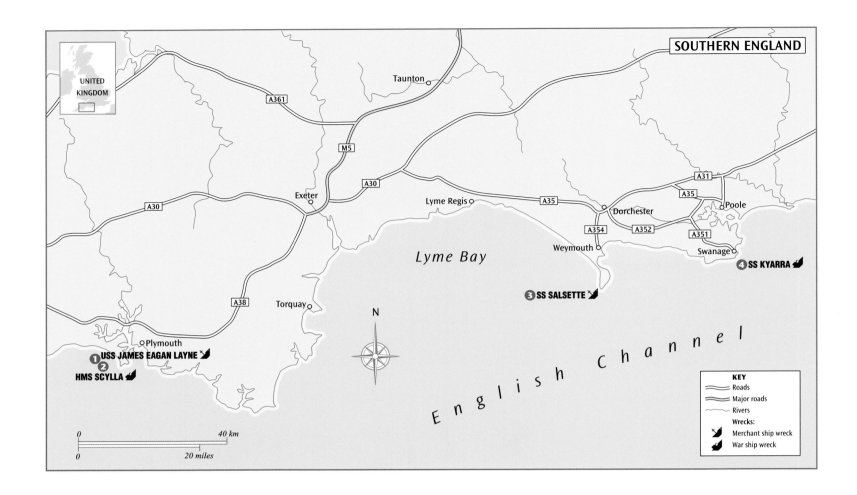

ENGLAND

USS JAMES EAGAN LAYNE ❶

Probably the most dived wreck in GB waters, the 7,176 ton *James Eagan Layne* was one of the 188 Liberty ships built by the Delta Shipbuilding Company of New Orleans at the Joshua Hendy Ironworks of Sunnyvale, California. With a length of 134m (441ft) and a beam of 17m (57ft), she was fitted with triple-expansion engines. One of 120 Liberty ships named after men of the American Merchant Marine who were killed in enemy action during the war, she was launched on 2 December 1944 by James Eagan Layne's widow, Marjorie. On her maiden voyage at the beginning of March

1945, the *James Eagan Layne* crossed the Atlantic to Barry Roads with her holds full of war supplies. She had joined Convoy BTC 103 en route to Ghent when she was attacked by U-boat U1195. A torpedo struck her just aft of the engine-room.

Admiralty tugs took her in tow but she sank 1.6km (1 mile) from Rame Head in Whitsand Bay at 22:30 on 21 March 1945. Salvage of guns and easily accessible equipment began immediately. More salvage was carried out by Icelandic and British companies after the war. Amateur divers have been visiting the vessel since 1954 – be warned that she gets very busy, even with HMS *Scylla* nearby.

Today the *James Eagan Layne* is permanently buoyed at the bow and lies upright, north-to-south from 8m (28ft) on the top of the bow to 26m (85ft) on the seabed, depending on the state of the tide. The top of the bow faces north at 8m (26ft). Most of the detached stern lies some 10m (33ft) to the southwest of where it should be. She can be dived at any state of the tide, but be careful on big spring tides. There is much to see, from wagon wheels to batteries, lots of anemones and large shoals of fish. The engine and war supplies that were once obscured by debris are now more visible, but be careful as the vessel is decaying fast.

HMS SCYLLA ❷

Bought in 2003 by the Plymouth-based National Marine Aquarium with £200,000 funding provided by the South West of England Regional Development Agency, HMS *Scylla* is Europe's first artificial diving reef. She was environmentally cleaned; snagging hazards were eliminated and doors welded shut or open before she was scuttled off Whitsand Bay in Cornwall on 27 March 2004. She lies about 700m (2,297ft) from the James Eagan Layne. Intended for marine research as well as diving, the gradual colonization of the *Scylla* by marine life will be constantly available via web-cam and the website.

The 2,500 tonne Leander class frigate HMS *Scylla* was built in the nearby Devonport Dockyard. She was 113m (371ft) long, with a beam of 13m (43ft). Launched on 8 August 1968, she was decommiss-ioned in 1993. Today she is lying almost upright with just a slight list to starboard. The bow faces south-west. Like the *James Eagan Layne*, she is an easy dive with little tide. She has buoys at the stern, amidships and bow. A frigate is more detailed to explore than a similar-sized merchant ship. With divers in mind, several holes have been cut in the hull, but the engine room has been sealed with concrete.

SS SALSETTE ❸

Another excellent wreck dive in Great Britain is the Peninsular & Oriental Steam Navigation Company's

5,842 ton SS *Salsette*, which was built by Caird & Company at Greenock in 1908. With a length of 134m (440ft) and a 16m (53ft) beam, she was a combined passenger/cargo vessel used to run the express mail service between Britain and India. Having just set out from London she was torpedoed on the starboard side by UB-40 in Lyme Bay, 11.5 nautical miles west of Portland Bill on 20 July 1917. She sank within 28 minutes.

Today she lies with a list of about 35 degrees to port and with the bow pointing north in 44m (144ft) of water with some scouring to 48m (157ft). It is 34m (112ft) to the starboard railings. An advanced dive subject to tidal currents, surface swell and mono-filament fishing lines and nets, it should be dived at slack water. A big ship, partially collapsed and fairly deep, it requires several dives to do it justice. There have been many good non-ferrous finds amid the luxury fittings. A large gun is still fixed to its mount above the upper deck and there are many holes that allow some great penetration for experienced divers, but be careful of the debris and the depth.

SS KYARRA ❹

'The ship that was made of brass' is what they called the 6,953 ton SS *Kyarra* when she was launched by Denny Bros in Dumbarton on 2 February 1903. Not only her portholes, but also many of her interior and exterior fittings were solid brass.

The combined passenger/cargo liner *Kyarra* was 126m (415ft) long and had a beam of 16m (52ft). She was registered in Fremantle, Australia, before World War I and plied the England-to-Australia run for the Australasian United Steam Navigation Co. The British Government requisitioned and armed her for war duties in October 1914. Despite service at Gallipoli and use as a hospital ship, she still carried a surprising amount of civilian cargo like perfume, champagne, silk and watches when on the Australian run. She sailed from Tilbury on 24 May 1918 and, in the early morning of 26 May, she was torpedoed amidships on her port side by UB-57 and sank quickly near Swanage.

Today the *Kyarra*'s rotting remains lie on her starboard side in 30m (98ft) of water with the port railing uppermost at roughly 23m (75ft). A large ship, partly intact with much to see, she can be very busy. The dive is not for novices and she must be dived at slack water. Be careful not to touch any puddles of liquid mercury spilled from the cargo. The stern has now broken off to leave debris and the rudder separated from the rest of the wreck. There are plenty of fish, but penetrate with care. The holes are small and broken and often are only large enough for one diver at a time.

REPUBLIC OF IRELAND

RMS LUSITANIA ❺

The 31,550 ton luxury Cunard liner RMS *Lusitania* was built by John Brown & Co Ltd. of Clydebank, Glasgow and launched on the River Clyde on 7 June 1906 by Mary, Lady Inverclyde. She was 239m (785ft) long, with a beam of 26.5m (88ft). Her four direct-drive Parsons steam turbines developed some 68,000 indicated horsepower and drove four propellers enabling a speed of 26.7 knots. She had accommodation for 563 first class, 464 second class and 1,138 third (steerage) class passengers. Construction was subsidized by loans from the British Government and in return the Admiralty could requisition her in times of war. At the onset of World War I in August 1914 the *Lusitania*, *Mauretania* and the newer 'sister ship' *Aquitania* were all officially requisitioned for war duties, but the *Lusitania* continued her regular transatlantic passenger services where she was the largest and fastest vessel of her time plying the route.

On 7 May 1915 she was carrying 1,257 passengers and 702 crew from New York to Liverpool when she was torpedoed 18km (11¼ miles) south-southwest of the Old Head of Kinsale, Southern Ireland, by the

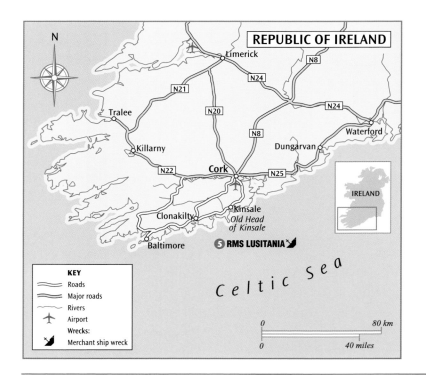

German submarine U-20. At 14:10 one torpedo hit the forward cargo hold and the Lusitania sank in 18 minutes. Over 1,200 people died. The fact that she was a passenger ship and the dead included 123 Americans, 291 women and 94 children, had much to do with America entering World War I in 1917.

The wreck, oriented roughly northeast to southwest, was first dived in 1935 by Englishman Jim Jarrett using a forerunner of the armoured one-atmosphere diving suit. The British Royal Navy dived her in 1954. In the late 1960s and early 1970s John Light, an American naval diver who then owned the wreck, dived her several times, but with limited bottom times. In 1982 a salvage operation, using Heliox and a diving bell, recovered her anchors and three of her four propellers. In 1993, the locator of the *Titanic*, Robert Ballard, surveyed her with submersibles and Remotely Operated Vehicles (ROVs).

The first visit by recreational technical divers was in 1994, when eight Britons led by Polly Tapson were joined by deep-wreck diving expert Gary Gentile and three of his friends from the East Coast of America. To dive to 93m (305ft), each diver's rig consisted of twin 15 litre (120cu ft) back-mounted cylinders containing Trimix, plus two side-mounted 10 litre (80cu ft) cylinders containing travel/decompression Nitrox, and each cylinder had a separate regulator. Nitrox 32, Nitrox 50 and pure oxygen were used for decompression. One pure oxygen cylinder per diver, each with its own regulator, was hung from bars at 6m (20ft), and the whole system could be detached to float in the current for stress-free final decompression.

The *Lusitania* was dived again in 1995, 1999 and in 2001 by a Starfish Enterprise team led by Mark Jones. This team, made up of 13 bottom-divers using six open-circuit Trimix rigs, one Cis-Lunar rebreather and six Buddy Inspiration rebreathers together with four cover-divers, worked with the owner Gregg Bemis Jr. on an archaeological survey as a precursor to raising and conserving artefacts. The wreck lies on her starboard side with the bow in good condition and draped in lost trawl nets. The stern is still recognizable as part of the ship, but the middle section is badly broken up.

There has been much unresolved conjecture over a second, larger explosion that occurred after the torpedo hit. One source says that it may have been coal dust in the boiler room's air. However, among the *Lusitania*'s cargo were '1248 cases of LIVE 3" shrapnel shells' and 90 tons of 'unrefrigerated butter and cheese destined for the Royal Navy Weapons Testing Establishment in Essex'.

SCOTLAND

SCAPA FLOW

The bay of Scapa Flow, in the Orkney Islands, covers some 190sq km (73 square miles), and is completely sheltered by a ring of protective islands. Scapa Flow offers the best wreck diving in Europe and ranks

among the top five diving areas of the world. There is more wreckage in Scapa Flow than in any other location on the planet. Long considered to be impregnable to attack, this deep, formidable, cold, natural harbour has served the fleets of warring nations since the time of the Vikings, the Knights of St John, the Spanish Armada and the Napoleonic and American Wars of Independence. At present Scapa Flow contains the wrecks of three German battleships; four light cruisers; five torpedo boats (small destroyers); a World War II destroyer (F2); one submarine; 27 large sections of remains and salvor's equipment; 32 blockships and two British battleships (the *Vanguard* and the *Royal Oak*); a further 16 known British wrecks and many other bits of wreckage are as yet unidentified.

At the end of World War I, the German High Seas Fleet was interned as part of the sanctions against Germany following her surrender. The

Above: Docking telegraph on the stern of the RMS *Lusitania*.

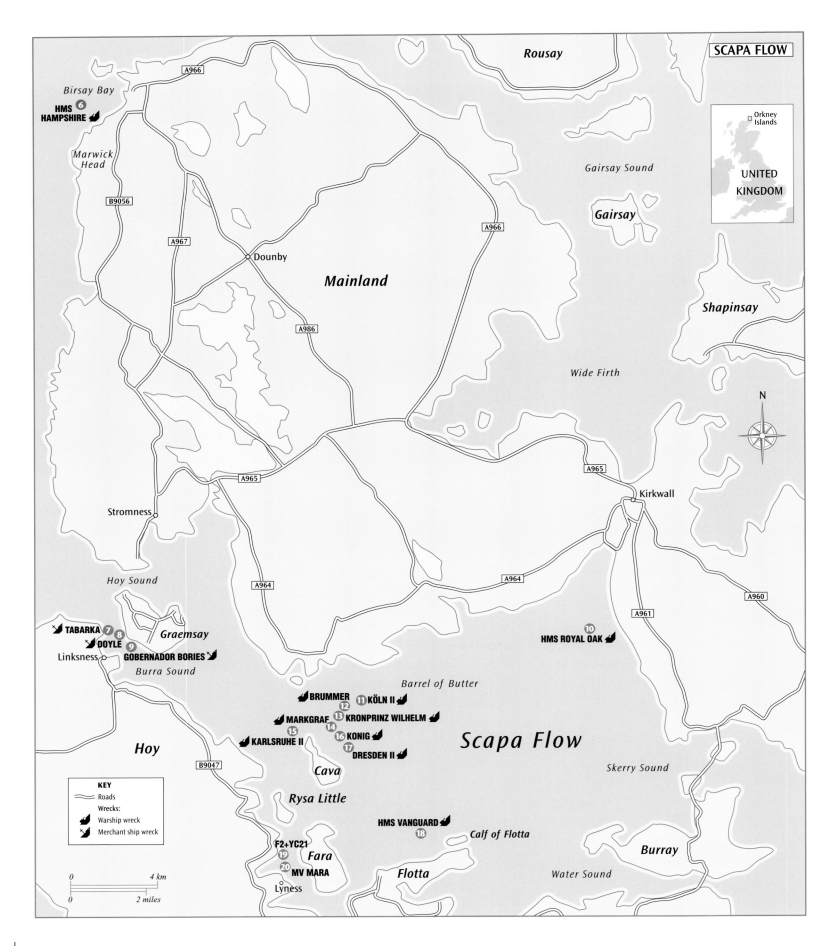

SCAPA FLOW

Orkney Islands

UNITED KINGDOM

Rousay

Birsay Bay

HMS 6
HAMPSHIRE

Marwick Head

A966

B9056

A967

Gairsay Sound

Gairsay

A966

Dounby

Mainland

Shapinsay

A986

Wide Firth

N

A965

A965

Kirkwall

Stromness

Hoy Sound

A964

A964

A961

A960

TABARKA 7 8
DOYLE 9
Linksness GOBERNADOR BORIES
Graemsay
Burra Sound

HMS ROYAL OAK 10

Barrel of Butter

BRUMMER 12 11 KÖLN II
13 KRONPRINZ WILHELM
MARKGRAF
15 14 KONIG
KARLSRUHE II 16
17 DRESDEN II

Scapa Flow

Skerry Sound

Hoy

B9047

Cava

Rysa Little

HMS VANGUARD
18

Calf of Flotta

Burray

F2+YC21
19
Fara
20 MV MARA
Lyness

Flotta

Water Sound

KEY
— Roads
Wrecks:
Warship wreck
Merchant ship wreck

0   4 km
0   2 miles

German ships were stripped of their armaments and, with only skeleton crews, were taken under armed escort to Scapa Flow, the main base of Britain's Home Fleet, until it could be decided what to do with them.

On Saturday, 21 June 1919, Admiral Ludwig von Reuter decided to save his country's honour and ordered the deliberate scuttling of the fleet. Within four hours, most of the German ships had sunk from view, while others were beached and many flipped upside down on their way to the seabed. The three deep battleships are the *König* (16) at a depth of 40m (131ft); *Kronprinz Wilhelm* (13) at a depth of 34m (112ft) and the *Markgraf* (14) at a depth 42m (138ft).

Although the German fleet now makes up the bulk of the wrecks that are accessible to divers, the most interesting of all the diveable ships in Scapa Flow are the blockships sunk at the entrance to Burra Sound. These are the *Doyle* (8), the *Gobernador Bories* (9) and the *Tabarka* (7). The *Inverlane*, once one of the most famous of all the blockships, has now completely broken up and is rarely visited.

Between dives, the dive boats often anchor on the jetty at Lyness, the former Naval Base on the Island of Hoy. Incidentally, nearby is the wreck of the F2, a World War II German torpedo boat and her salvage barge, the YC-21, sunk in 1968 (19). The salvage company had just removed a set of guns from the F2 and had tied tight onto the stricken vessel at low tide. The crew went off to celebrate their good fortune at being able to raise the guns and left their booty to a rising tide which, lo and behold, sank their barge and their booty – now making two very nice divable ships (and both with guns).

There are three designated war graves in the vicinity (where no diving is allowed at all, unless you have direct permission from the Admiralty). HMS *Hampshire* (6) lies at a depth 68m (223ft) off west Orkney near Marwick Head. This is where Lord Kitchener lost his life along with 650 other poor souls on 5 June 1916. HMS *Vanguard* (18) lying at a depth of 34m (112ft) in southern Scapa Flow, was sunk by a mystery explosion on 9 July 1917, taking 804 men with her. HMS *Royal Oak* (10), lying at a depth of 32m (105ft), is where 833 men died. She was sunk by the U-47 commanded by Gunther Prien on 14 October 1939.

Twenty years after the German fleet was scuttled, on the night of 14 October 1939, the 183m (600ft) battleship HMS *Royal Oak* was at anchor in the sheltered bay of Scapa Flow. Her duties were to protect Kirkwall and the British fleet from aerial attack. Scapa Flow was considered impenetrable because of the narrow passages between the reefs and islands. Likely attack would be expected only from the skies. However, nobody told this to Günther Prien, the commander of the submarine U-47, who stealthily approached Scapa Flow through the only navigable waterway at Kirk Sound, to the east. At this time, the entrance channels between the eastern islands were tentatively blocked by abandoned merchant shipping collectively called blockships. In what is considered by many to be one of the most daring episodes of naval history, the U-47 sank the *Royal Oak* during the dead of night.

The ship is now a designated war grave and is protected by Navy Law. Diving on her is strictly forbidden, as a result of which she is the ship most divers want to visit. HMS *Royal Oak* now rests on her starboard side, but almost upside down at 135 degrees to the vertical in 29m (95ft) of water. Her keel is now encrusted in soft corals, sea stars, sponges and anemones and surrounded by schools of juvenile Haddock and Saithe. The spotting top is still fairly intact; it stretches out from the hull and lies near the Admiral's steam barge, which was dragged under when the *Royal Oak* sank and could not be deployed to assist in the rescue of her sailors.

The giant barrels of her 380mm (15 inch) guns are still embedded in the sea floor and actually support the larger part of the ship. Open hatches and companionways and links of her anchor chain, each over 1m (40 inches) long, dropping to the seabed are testimony to the rapid sinking of the ship. Anti-aircraft guns still have their ammunition intact in their racks and the smaller 150mm (6 inch) and 100 mm (4 inch) guns stretch out into the Orkney waters, completely covered in a mantle of Plumose Anemones, sponges and sea stars.

As a direct result of the sinking of the *Royal Oak*, Winston Churchill visited Orkney and ordered the permanent construction of causeways between Orkney Mainland, Lamb Holm, Glims Holm, Burray and South Ronaldsay. He insisted that this type of attack should never happen again. To implement these measures, over 2,000 Italian prisoners of war, captured during the North African campaign, worked alongside local contractors to permanently block the sea lanes and build new roads between all of the islands. These roads became collectively known as 'The Churchill Barriers'.

THE TOP TEN DIVEABLE WRECKS OF SCAPA FLOW

The above list is purely a personal opinion. Top of the list is the *Doyle*. This is the best British shipwreck I have even been lucky enough to dive. Built in Troon, Scotland, in 1907, this former 1,761 ton coastal freighter was sunk in its present position in Burra Sound as a blockship in 1940. The ship's aspect is completely open and she has settled on her port side. Her bows and stern are relatively intact and her propeller is covered in tiny Plumose Anemones. The wooden parts of her three decks have rotted away, leaving the metal ribs and all sections of the ship still robust enough to allow full access to divers. Ballan Wrasse, conger eels and schools of juvenile Haddock and Saithe inhabit the wreck. The starboard side of the exposed hull is covered in anemones, tubeworms and sponges.

Photographically and time wise, the *Gobernador Boreis* and the *Tabarka* (and the *Doyle* for that matter) are superb. They are also the most accessible

THE TOP TEN DIVEABLE WRECKS OF SCAPA FLOW

	VESSEL	TYPE	DATE SUNK
1	**DOYLE (8)**	(Blockship)	**1940**
2	**GOBERNADOR BOREIS (9)**	(Blockship)	**1915**
3	**TABARKA (7)**	(Blockship)	**1944**
4	**CÖLN II (11)**	(German light cruiser)	**1919**
5	**KARLSRUHE II (15)**	(German light cruiser)	**1919**
6	**BRUMMER (12)**	(German light cruiser)	**1919**
7	**DRESDEN II (17)**	(German light cruiser)	**1919**
8	**MARKGRAF (14)**	(German battleship)	**1919**
9	**F2 + YC21 (19)**	(German torpedo boat and salvage barge)	**1945** **1968**
10	**MV MARA (20)**	(Former dive boat)	**1999**

wrecks. The four German light cruisers come next as they sit far enough off the seabed, lying on their sides, which allows for a little extra time for exploration. The 5,354 ton *Karlsruhe II* (15) gets top marks for several reasons. Her starboard deck comes to as shallow as 15m (49ft) and the seabed at the stern is only 28m (92ft), making her the shallowest of all the German light cruisers. She is well broken up now and in the past few years has settled into the seabed even more, gradually sinking into the mud. Towards the rear of the ship, her guns are now only just visible and the anchor hanging off the stern has almost disappeared, when once it was over 6m (20ft) above. Her forward guns are now on the seabed. In general the ship is much the worse for wear. However, she still has the most marine life and is excellent for exploring at leisure.

I have only included one battleship, as all the others are well broken up and are considered quite dangerous now; divers should not be tempted to enter the ships at any time. The last two are somewhat of a prize. The F2 and the salvage barge, attached to her by rope, are both great for photography in shallower water. The MV *Mara* (20) was a former dive boat which had been abandoned and

Opposite: The view looking upwards through the interior of the *Doyle* is simply stunning, with the hull plates covered in kelp and the interior sections covered in soft corals and hydroids.

gradually started to sink while berthed at Lyness; it was decided to sink her in the vicinity of the F2 and the YC-21 salvage barge.

Scapa Flow has acquired an unfounded notoriety over the years. It is true that divers have lost their lives here over the years, but this is the same for every popular diving destination. Nowadays, divers are more informed, better trained and have the latest diving computers to guide them through the complicated variables of multi-level diving.

Many divers still assume that you can only explore the German fleet wrecks using Nitrox, Trimix or rebreathers, and that all of the dives should be treated as decompression dives, only to be dived by super-qualified divers. This type of diving can possibly put more undue stress on the diver; it considerably extends the time to be spent in the water and it can increase the susceptibility to hypothermia, which affects motor functions. Many divers are attracted to the 'technical' side of deep diving, but the need to attend courses and buy the equipment will not outweigh the fact that the larger battleships are not only in very deep, dark water, they have also been deteriorating steadily since 1919, and they are all upside down, with few recognizable features and can be potentially dangerous to explore any further.

Diving in Scapa Flow can be as easy or as difficult as you want to make it. Novice divers can have a great diving holiday, and indeed many visitors gain their first diving qualification through the excellent diving schools on the island. The shallowest part of the *Karlsruhe II* is only in 15m (49ft) and the seabed is less than 30m (98ft). All of the motor torpedo boats and blockships are in less than 18m (59ft), and are quite possibly some of the best shallow shipwrecks in the world. All the blockships and German light cruisers are achievable for novice divers (under supervision), who can dive alongside those super-qualified, mixed gas divers on over 70 per cent of the same shipwrecks.

There is a museum nearby on Hoy, with an excellent display of artefacts relating to the two world wars. The museums in both Stromness and Kirkwall are also well worth a visit. Kirkwall Cathedral has a special commemoration on HMS *Royal Oak*.

SS HISPANIA ❶

The 1,337 ton, 80.5m (264ft) Swedish steamship *Hispania* was built in 1912 by the Antwerp Engineering Company Ltd. Her final voyage began when she left Liverpool loaded with a cargo of steel asbestos and rubber, bound for Varberg in Sweden on Friday 17 December 1954. The weather was poor as she steamed north through the Irish Sea and the North Channel, so Captain Ivan Dahn decided to take a route that would give some protection from the weather by sailing between the islands off the Scottish west coast. She came into the Sound of Mull on 18 December and made her way up the narrow channel towards Tobermory Bay where they could shelter for the rest of the night. Due to a local thunderstorm that night, visibility was atrocious, and it was almost pitch black. With almost no land reference, the *Hispania* struck the rocky outcrop of Sgeir Mor. Her holds filled with water and it was evident that the ship was going to sink very quickly. The crew of 21 calmly took to the lifeboats before she sank, except for Captain Dahn who, despite the pleadings of the crew, could not be persuaded to leave and in the sad, age-old tradition, went down with his ship.

The *Hispania*'s cargo was salvaged in the 1950s, and in 1957 a wire sweep was carried out by the Royal Navy to aid navigation by other ships in the Sound of Mull. Otherwise, she is as intact as when she sank in December 1954. The ship sits upright, with a list to starboard, in 30m (98ft) of water. Located just inshore of the red channel marker buoy, the *Hispania* is normally buoyed and therefore very easily located with her bow pointing due west towards the Mull shore. Depths on the deck range

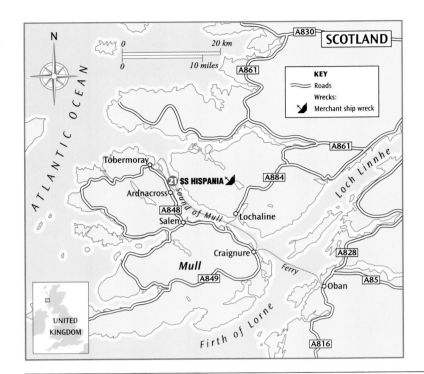

from 15–21m (49–69ft), with the holds and engine room at 23m (75ft). A dive on the *Hispania* normally begins amidships, at the bottom of the shot line, and then the diver should proceed towards the stern, using the wreck to shelter from the current. A spare propeller can be seen, slotted into a hole on the stern deck. Much of the deck gear is intact, including some impressive winches to the front of each cargo hold. You should drop over the port side of the stern and closely examine the hull for nudibranchs as you swim around to the starboard side.

The *Hispania* is a spectacular wreck with almost every square inch of her metal surface covered in sea life, particularly the dwarf species of Plumose Anemone which come in white, green and orange colours. The wreck has a fairly considerable list to starboard, and a number of pulleys, winch gear and masts have rolled off the deck to the seabed, creating homes for large congers and fish. The almost inevitable good visibility encountered at the end of the flood tide makes this one of the best scenic wreck

dives in Scotland. As a result of this she is one of the most popular wreck dives, but she is virtually intact with companionways, handrails and doors still in place. Only the wooden structures have rotted away and any brass fittings have, of course, disappeared. Otherwise a swim through her bridge or into the cavernous holds or engine room is almost like a walk round a ship afloat.

Puffin Dive Centre has now purchased the wreck of the SS *Hispania*. By doing so, it has been able to inhibit any salvaging or unauthorized taking of artefacts from the wreck, which means more for divers to see. This also ensures that mooring buoys and lines are kept to a good standard, making it easier for visiting divers.

Above: The *Hispania* is perhaps one of the most scenic shipwrecks on the Scottish west coast. Now totally smothered in small orange and white plumose anemones, it is very colourful.

SOUTH AFRICA

By Jason Martin

South Africa's long coastline and the turbulent Antarctic (Southern) Ocean have claimed more than their fair share of shipping in the five centuries or so since European seafarers began to round the Cape of Good Hope in search of the riches of the East. There are over 3,700 known shipwrecks along the South African coast. Ongoing research and exploration is yielding fascinating information about many of these ships. The Cape Peninsula and surrounding waters contain the sites of no less than 450 shipwrecks – ranging from 17th-century Dutch East Indiamen to massive modern bulk carriers. This variety, together with the natural beauty of the area, makes Cape Town one of the world's best wreck diving destinations.

Opposite: Now home to a variety of marine life, the SS *Maori* is one of Cape Town's most popular shipwrecks.

Southeast of the Cape Peninsula is Cape Agulhas, the southernmost tip of Africa, on the 20°E meridien and official boundary beween the Indian and Atlantic Oceans.

The southern tip of the Cape Peninsula is Cape Point. To the north on its west coast is Table Bay, the original 'tavern of the seas' where the Atlantic Ocean deposits its cold, nutrient-rich waters. To the east of the peninsula is False Bay, with its teeming fish shoals, mammal migration and penguin habitation. The prevailing winds of the region are seasonal. In summer, a strong southeasterly onshore wind blows in False Bay, but flattens and clears the waters in Table Bay. In winter rain-bearing northwesterly winds devastate Table Bay, but clear and flatten False Bay.

MAORI BAY ②

To the south of Cape Town lies the suburb of Hout Bay, home to an active fishing fleet. A short trip from Hout Bay, running northwest round the Sentinel and past Seal Island, lie the remains of some five shipwrecks. The most popular of these is the *Maori*, which lends its name to this popular dive spot. The bay lies exposed to the northwesterly winds and reveals the remains of the *Bos 400*, a giant floating crane barge that came to grief on the 27 June 1994. Most of the remains of the *Bos 400* lie above the surface. The ship, with its massive helicopter platform and boom listing to 20 degrees, can clearly be seen from Clifton Beach some 10km (6 miles) away, forming a blemish on this otherwise picture-perfect coastline. The *Bos 400* was being towed in a northwesterly gale when she broke her lines and drifted inshore to her current resting place. With her keel firmly embedded on the granite boulders, there is very little risk of the vessel collapsing. What makes this a great dive is the sheer size of the structure: you can dive right underneath the wreck to a depth of 22m (72ft). By navigating your way through the boulders you can swim up into the hull, which makes this a most exciting and technical dive. On the

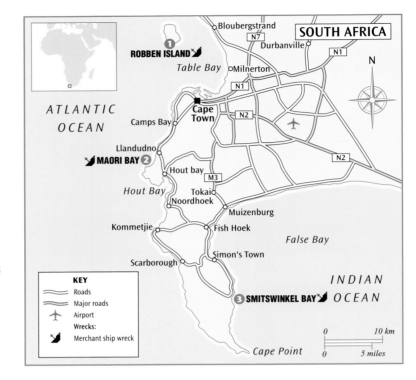

seabed divers can search the deck plates, among which thousands of crayfish (rock lobster) have made their home, since many ships' fittings were lost during the sinking. The wreck has been salvaged, but has not been made safe. More importantly, the seabed below the *Bos 400* is home to the remains of the *Oakburn*, the oldest wreck in Maori Bay.

The *Oakburn*, a British cargo steamer, was en route to Sydney from New York carrying railway equipment, instruments, glassware, oil and paper when she ran aground in fog on the southwesterly tip of Maori Bay on 21 May 1906. Although the main structure of the vessel has all but disappeared, the main boilers, steel ribs and keel can be seen intertwined with a jumbled mess of steel. What makes this dive interesting is the fact that divers can dive on two wrecks at once, one intact, the other not, and although the *Oakburn* is protected by South Africa's national heritage authority, it is still quite possible to come across 99-year-old artefacts, although it is illegal to remove them. The rocky outcrops of Die Middelmas and Oud Schip guard the northwesterly side of Maori Bay, and are the final resting place of two fishing trawlers that sank in the early 1980s. Both vessels have broken up completely, and have been consumed by the seafloor, where brightly coloured anemones, sea urchins, sponges and kelp have covered their bare remains. With an abundance of flora, marine fauna abounds. Common sand hermit crabs, octopuses and West Coast rock lobsters patrol the sandy seabed, while fish such as Geelbek, White Stumpnose, Hottentot, Blacktail and other species nervously keep an eye out for the ever-present Cape Fur Seal.

Finally, Maori Bay wouldn't be Maori Bay without the wreck of the same name. The *Maori* was a 5,317 tonne British steamer built in 1893 by Swan & Hunter of Newcastle, and was owned by the Shaw Savill Company. On 5 August 1909, while under the command of Captain G. Nicole, the *Maori* was on her way to New Zealand from London with a cargo of waterpipes, crockery and explosives. Caught in fog and heavy drizzle, the *Maori* ran ashore. The ship's stern rammed the southern point of the bay. Facing worsening weather, the crew and passengers made their way ashore, leaving the *Maori* to her fate. Thirty-two lives were lost in the disaster.

Today the *Maori* is Cape Town's most popular wreck dive. The wreck lies suspended over large boulders, with her expansion engine visible from the surface at 6m (20ft). The deck on the stern is at water level, angling down to 21m (69ft) at her bow.

Below: The area around Robben Island is another place where shipwrecks are common in the bay.

Although the wreck has been extensively salvaged – with one salvor even using explosives to free up cargo – the hull is in pretty good condition, allowing divers to brave a swim beneath her keel from one side of the ship to the other. The annual onslaught of winter weather sees the slow degradation of the site, but the wreckage is home to thousands of crayfish, sea anemones, shy sharks, octopuses and Cape Fur Seals that come to feast on the profusion of fish life. The *Maori* is the perfect Atlantic Cape dive as it caters for all levels of diver certification.

SMITSWINKEL BAY ❸

False Bay's premium wreck site is Smitswinkel Bay, located roughly 12km (7½miles) south of Simon's Town. The bay is the resting place of five vessels purposely sunk by the South African Navy in the early 1970s to form artificial reefs. With depths ranging between 35 and 40m (115–131ft) to the sand, the remains of the SAS *Transvaal*, SAS *Good Hope* – both decommissioned frigates – the *Rockeater* (a diamond dredger), and two fishing vessels – the *Princess Elizabeth* and the *Oratava* – lie within easy swimming distance of each other. Although these vessels remain ghostly intact and upright figures of their former past, it is their new role in the environment that attracts divers to these shadowy depths. There are hulls covered with stony and soft corals in whites, reds, orange, mauve and pink; overhangs teeming with fish; and the thrill of encountering some of the Cape's bigger pelagic fish, since schools of yellowtail and cob frequent the bay. Other attractions are the migratory Southern Right Whales in summer, the energetic Dusky Dolphins all year round and, occasionally, a shark. Able divers visiting the depths of the upright frigates can swim from one vessel to the next. The depths of these wrecks limit the dive to advanced divers only. The wrecks have not been made safe (or buoyed), but the state of the wrecks is such that, unless seriously penetrated, there is very little risk of entrapment.

ROBBEN ISLAND ❶

Politically, Robben Island is famous as the place where Nelson Mandela was imprisoned. Environmentally, the island is a place of natural beauty and is a World Heritage Site. Historically, the island is key to the isolation of the unwanted, a place of solitude, a piece of Africa detached from the mainland. Today Robben Island is also an untouched archaeological treasure trove of maritime heritage dating back to the early 1600s. Located roughly 11km (7 miles) offshore in Table Bay, the island played a major role in the development of the Cape. Extending 1.5km (1 mile) from the island into the Atlantic, archaeologists have found evidence of up to 60 different wreck sites. This area includes the southwesterly *Whale Rock*, which doesn't quite break the surface and is therefore mostly invisible to shipping. Thanks to the security measures in place on the island during its time as a political prison, the wreck sites have inadvertently been protected, so it is no surprise that some of the wrecks date to as far back as the 1600s. The earliest was the *Yeanger van Horne*, which was wrecked in 1611. While diving a 20th-century cargo carrier, one is likely to come across the remains of a wooden hull. With an abundance of history, the wrecks surrounding the island – from sailing yachts to fishing trawlers, cargo carriers, research vessels, salvage tugs, East Indian Company galleons, schooners and wooden barques – lie waiting to be discovered.

Opposite: There are many popular shipwrecks in South African waters.

NAUTICAL ARCHAEOLOGICAL SOCIETY (NAS)

The Nautical Archaeological Society is a UK-based agency that educates sport divers in the fine art of maritime archaeology. When visiting South Africa, divers have the opportunity to work hand in hand with trained professionals while surveying untouched shipwrecks. The national heritage organization, South African Heritage Resource Agency (SAHRA), works with local wreck-diving outfit Wreckseekers and the National Survey of Underwater Heritage. Divers can be trained as NAS part 1 divers, giving them instant access to sensitive wreck sites such as those in Table Bay and around Robben Island. Training, however, must be based on education, respect and a genuine desire to solve age-old mysteries.

MEDITERRANEAN SEA

MALTA

By Lawson Wood

Malta's strategic location in the southern central Mediterranean is undoubtedly the common factor for so many wrecks to be found here. Many of them are casualties of the two world wars, and most are in very deep water and well offshore. Until the introduction of mixed gas and rebreathers, all of these superb wrecks were only explored on air, with divers regularly enduring nitrogen narcosis and a risk of the 'bends' to further their knowledge in their explorations.

Opposite: Divers surround the remains of the fuselage of the Bristol Beaufighter.

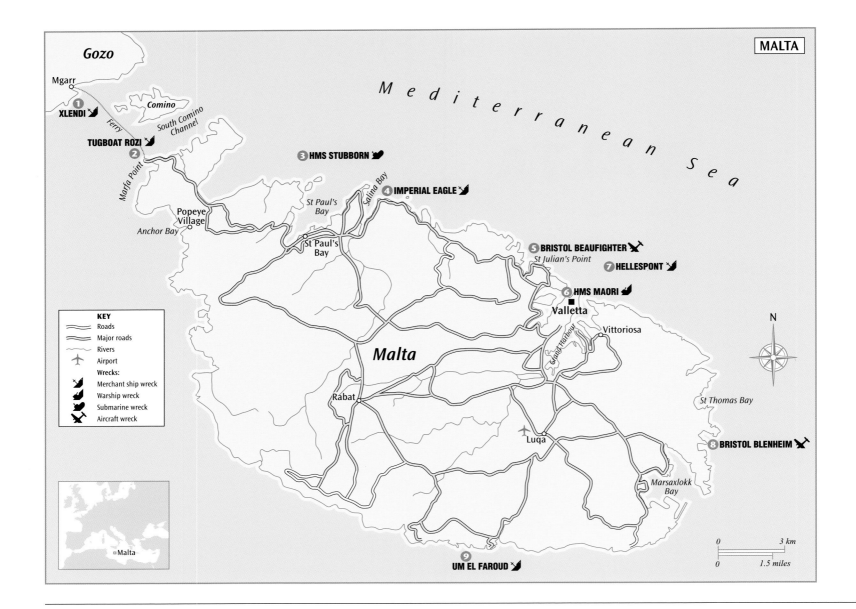

KEY
- Roads
- Major roads
- Rivers
- Airport
- Wrecks:
  - Merchant ship wreck
  - Warship wreck
  - Submarine wreck
  - Aircraft wreck

Gozo

Mgarr

① XLENDI

Comino

② TUGBOAT ROZI

Marfa Point

Ferry

South Comino Channel

③ HMS STUBBORN

Salina Bay

④ IMPERIAL EAGLE

St Paul's Bay

Popeye Village

Anchor Bay

St Paul's Bay

⑤ BRISTOL BEAUFIGHTER

St Julian's Point

⑦ HELLESPONT

⑥ HMS MAORI

Valletta

Vittoriosa

Grand Harbour

Malta

Rabat

Luqa

St Thomas Bay

⑧ BRISTOL BLENHEIM

Marsaxlokk Bay

⑨ UM EL FAROUD

Mediterranean Sea

MALTA

N

□ Malta

0   3 km

0   1.5 miles

No stranger to siege conditions over the centuries, the Maltese islands suffered enormously from sustained Axis air naval attacks during World War II. The people of the islands were awarded the George Cross for 'a heroism and devotion that will long be famous in history'. The award was made by King George VI to the Governor of Malta by letter, dated 15 April 1942.

Strategically, Valletta Harbour was the focus for many of the attacks by the German and Italian air forces and Italian Navy during the war. Valletta has six diveable wreck sites, including HMS *Maori* and the Carolito barge – ideal for trainee divers. Other wrecks accessible are the Tent Peg Wreck, MV *Odile* and HMS *Jersey*.

These World War II shipwrecks are all well documented, but there have been a few interesting recent finds, particularly of military aircraft. There is a fairly intact Bristol Blenheim light bomber to the south of the island, near Marsaxlokk. A Bristol

Beaufighter (a twin-engined fighter), lies upside down and close to the shore near St Julians. Both these wrecks are at a depth of only 42m (138ft). Wreckage of an Italian seaplane is also in the vicinity, and a Spitfire fighter was recently discovered.

Malta also has some deep wrecks, such as HMS *Stubborn*, an intact submarine lying in 60m (197ft); *Le Polynesien* from World War I at the same depth; HMS *Southwold* in 70m (230ft); and the *Hellespont* (also from World War I), which is situated near a World War II German E-Boat or *Schnell Boot* in only 36m (118ft). These sites are now being visited more frequently, since deep diving is now very much part of the Maltese diving scene, with many local divers and visitors using Trimix and rebreathers.

I hesitate to call deliberately sunk ships artificial reefs, since they are really only diver attractions. Yes, they do become covered in marine life; but research has shown that they do not necessarily help a reef; rather, they may only remove the burden of divers from an over-dived reef. Large wrecks attract large predatory fish and these can decimate the population of reef fish on a nearby reef. The new shipwrecks sunk as diver attractions are the *Imperial Eagle*, *Rozi*, *Um el Faroud*, two former tugboats and three retired inter-island ferries.

The remains of all of these former vessels of war, aircraft and new diver attractions are now colonized by an amazing array of marine life, including tubeworms, sponges, hydroids, nudibranchs and tiny corals. All of them are surrounded by small schools of fish that are preyed upon by scorpionfish, various groupers and hunter-pelagics such as amberjacks and dentex.

BRISTOL BLENHEIM ❽
On 13 December 1941, a Bristol Blenheim Mark IV of Number 18 Squadron serial #Z7858 (code M) was one of a squadron of bombers sent out on a raid to attack enemy merchantmen. Soon after leaving Luqa airfield this aircraft was attacked by an Italian

Macchi. With her port engine disabled and propeller shot off, the pilot, Sgt Frank Jury, accompanied by air-gunner Sgt Dennis Mortimer and navigator Tom Black, managed to bring the aircraft back to Malta, but were unable to land. They headed out over Marsaxlokk and decided to ditch the bomber, after jettisoning her payload, near a *dghajsa* or Maltese fishing boat. All three crew managed to escape with little injury. The wreck lies off the southeast coast, 800m (875 yards) due east of Xorb il-Ghagin, in a depth of 41m (135ft).

The Bristol Blenheim is still lying upright, but is deteriorating quite badly now. Most of the central fuselage and both wings are intact, as are the starboard engine and propeller. However, the tail and the cockpit are both gone. Her undercarriage is now exposed and you can see them retracted inside the wing casings to aid her streamlined flight profile. The seabed is fairly clean around her, with patches of Posidonia sea-grass, and the area abounds with small chromis and Bogue. The site is exposed so it can be choppy with some current.

BRISTOL BEAUFIGHTER ❺
The Beaufighter 'N' was just one of many casualties lost in the protection of the islands during World War II. Together with others from No. 272 Squadron, the aircraft left Malta on 17 March 1943 to escort nine Beaufort torpedo bombers on a raid against Point Stelo. Commanded by Sgt Donald Frazee, with Sgt Sandray as observer, the aircraft developed mechanical problems soon after take-off. It started to vibrate rapidly and quickly began to lose altitude. Unable to reach the safety of the airfield, the crew had no alternative but to ditch the fighter. The aircraft struck the water at over 160kph (100mph). Both crewmen escaped the wreck, which apparently stayed afloat for only about 15 seconds. They were picked up by Maltese *dghajsas* before further help arrived. The aircraft now lies upside down on a clean, sandy seabed, 900m (984 yards) offshore to the

Above: The remains of the front of a Bristol Blenheim engine and propeller.

northwest of St Julian's Point. A great deal of the underside of the fuselage has rotted away, and much of the aeroplane is buried under the sand. However, both wings are still fairly intact. Also, both the undercarriage frames and, now shredded, tyres stick up from their wing positions behind the engines. The starboard engine cowling is gone, with the propeller partly buried, except for one blade that stands upright. The starboard propeller broke off during impact and now lies around 30m (98ft) away from the aircraft. Divers are able to inspect the undercarriage and machine-gun assemblies that are covered in a fine patina of marine growth. The wreck site is surrounded by thousands of chromis.

With a maximum depth of 38m (125ft), the site is exposed so it can be choppy with some current.

IMPERIAL EAGLE ❹

The 45m (148ft) *Imperial Eagle*, with a beam of 9m (30ft), was a former passenger ferry modified to carry cars that operated between Gozo and Malta. She was sunk as an artificial reef and proposed conservation area on 19 July 1999 offshore between Qawra Point and Qretjen Point. The average depth is 28m (92ft), and the maximum depth 42m (138ft). This site is regarded as a long deep dive in an undersea valley. First stop is the 3m (10ft), 13 ton fibreglass-covered concrete statue of Christ that was made to commemorate the Pope's visit to Malta in 1981. It was placed underwater near St Paul's Island during the visit, after it had been blessed by the Pope himself. Unfortunately, due to poor visibility and a lack of fish in that area, it was rarely visited by divers. In May 2000 it was moved to its present location, 15m (49ft) away from the wreck of the *Imperial Eagle*. This forms a secondary underwater attraction in the area. Divers then proceed to the bow of the ship. Sitting intact and upright and relatively new, her spoked steering wheel is quite photogenic. She has a fine patina of algae and is home to many wrasse, chromis, Bogue and groupers. The sides of the surrounding underwater valley are covered in Posidonia sea grass. This is another exposed site so it can be choppy, with some currents.

HMS MAORI ❻

HMS *Maori* was launched in 1937 and saw considerable action in the Mediterranean, being involved, with the HMS *Dorsetshire*, in the sinking of the *Bismarck*. During a massive aerial bombardment on 12 February 1942, she received a direct hit and quickly sank. Now completely wrecked in Valletta harbour, the *Maori* is accessed from the shore, down

the steps followed by a 30m (98ft) swim down the rocky slope. The vessel's bow is gone, as is the entire stern. Part of the bridge is accessible above the muddy seabed of the harbour, but beware of the numerous live shells sticking out of the wreckage and mud. Also look out for overhead boat traffic. The average depth is 24m (79ft), while the maximum depth 28m (92ft).

HMS STUBBORN ❸

World War II Submarine HMS *Stubborn* was deliberately sunk by the Royal Navy on 30 April 1946 as an ASDIC/sonar target for training purposes. She sits almost upright and intact northwest of St Paul's Bay in 60m (197ft) of water with an average depth of

Left: The *Maori* is accessed from the shore followed by a 30m (98ft) swim.

54m (177ft). The wreck is located offshore with very little marine life around her, but is covered in algae and small sponges and is an incredible site.

UM EL FAROUD ❾

The 10,000 ton Libyan oil tanker *Um El Faroud* was built in 1969 by Smith Dock Co. Ltd., Middlesborough, England. She had a length of 109.53m (359ft) and a beam of 15.5m (51ft). She was owned by the General National Maritime Transport Company, Tripoli (GNMTC). Until 1 February 1995 she operated between Italy and Libya carrying refined fuel. On the night of 3 February 1995 she was docked at No. 3 Dock of Malta Dry-docks when an explosion occurred in No. 3 centre tank. Nine shipyard workers were killed. The vessel was a total write-off. She lay in Valletta Harbour until it was decided to scuttle her in September 1998 as a diving

Above: The *Um el Faroud* sits upright, in two distinct parts, and is classed as one of the best shore wreck dives in the Maltese Islands.

attraction and artificial reef. Now sitting upright on a sandy seabed at 36m (118ft), she has split amidships into two sections. The shallowest part of the wreck is above the bridge at 15m (49ft). A memorial plaque commemorates the men who died in the explosion.

TUGBOAT ROZI ❷

West of Cirkewwa Point the harbour tugboat *Rozi* was deliberately sunk in 1991 as an attraction for visitors in glass-bottomed boat tours. Now it is one of the main shore dives for divers and sits perfectly upright on a sandy bottom at 36m (118ft). The engines and propeller were removed before she was sunk. Covered in fine algae and small sponges, the vessel is negotiable on a single dive and is now home to thousands of fish, with chromis, bream and sand smelt being the predominant species. Nearby, the Posidonia sea-grass beds are home to cuttlefish and pipefish. The wreck is popular and gets busy because it is one of only three wrecks which divers can do as a shore dive. For experienced divers the *Rozi* is a superb night dive.

XLENDI ❶

South of Ghajnsielem, west of Mgarr Harbour the 1,123 ton, 77m (253ft) MV *Xlendi* was a roll-on roll-off (Ro-Ro) ferry built in 1955 in Denmark. She was acquired by Gozo Channel Company in 1970 and worked between Cirkewwa, Valletta and Mgarr Harbour, until retired from service in 1997 as part of a cost-cutting exercise. She languished in Valletta Harbour in Malta while negotiations took place to determine her fate. Finally, on Friday 12 November 1999, the *Xlendi* was deliberately sunk as a diving attraction. However, the sinking did not go to plan and she turned over. As a Ro-Ro ferry, with both stern and bows identical, each with a propeller and rudder (she was nicknamed the coffin due to her shape), it is difficult to say whether she lies on her port or starboard side, but the *Xlendi* is now upside down and partly supported by her funnel and collapsed masts. The cargo bay of the ship is open, but collapsing slowly, and only suitably qualified divers may be able to swim all the way through her. This is a deep dive, but well worth the effort. The maximum depth is 48m (157ft).

The *Xlendi* can be accessed by boat, and it can also be reached by car down a rough farm track. A new car park has been created for divers close to the water's edge, as well as a set of ladders to aid exit.

HELLESPONT ❼

Built for His Majesty's Government of the United Kingdom by Earle's Shipbuilding and Engineering Company of Hull, the 45m (146½ft) paddle-wheel tug *Hellespont* was launched on 10 May 1910. From 1922 the vessel was based in Malta as a supply boat around the naval yards. On the night of 7 September 1940 she was bombed and damaged by an Italian aircraft, and was mothballed. When she was bombed again on 6 April 1942, her bow was completely destroyed. After the war, the Maltese authorities decided to clear the harbours and shipping lanes of all sunken craft and other debris. The *Hellespont* was raised, towed out to sea and sunk off Grand Harbour, where she now sits upright, completely embedded in the seabed.

The vessel's stern is intact and her rudder can still be seen, but her propeller is under the silt and rocks. One of her boilers lies off to the side and both paddle-wheels have long since disintegrated. However, the paddle-wheel driveshafts still remain intact. A large capstan has now collapsed through the rotten, wooden aft decks, and the entire wreck has become a tangled mess and confusion as it slowly settles and comes apart. Old fishing lines and some nets are snagged on the superstructure. Care, as always, should be taken when diving old wrecks at such a depth.

This is an exposed site, so it can be choppy with some current. The average depth is 35m (115ft) and the maximum depth 40m (131ft).

CYPRUS

By Jack Jackson

WRECK FEATURED
★MV ZENOBIA

The third largest island in the Mediterranean after Sicily and Sardinia, Cyprus has many wrecks, but the *Zenobia* tops the list. In fact, to many divers the *Zenobia* is Cyprus diving, and the main reason for their visit. Because the wreck is so large and no one is allowed to remove artefacts, divers often make more than four dives on it.

Opposite: A diver swimming by the massive wreck of the MV *Zenobia*.

MV ZENOBIA ❶

The 172.02m (564ft) MV *Zenobia* was built by Kockums AB Shipbuilding Company of Malmö, Sweden, in 1979. The roll-on roll-off ferry had a 23.04m (75ft) beam and a gross tonnage of over 10,000 tons. She was powered by two seven-cylinder diesel engines producing 18,760 brake horsepower, giving a maximum speed of 21.5 knots. Both propellers had controllable pitch and there was an additional propeller, positioned forward, to facilitate docking.

On 4 May 1980 the *Zenobia* sailed for the Middle East on her maiden voyage. Mid-way between Crete and Athens, she started to list to port as her computerized ballast system developed a fault, pumping too much water into some ballast tanks. She pulled into Piraeus to pump out the water and the problem was thought to have been solved. However, on the 3 June, while anchored in Larnaca Bay, the problem returned.

On the 4 June the *Zenobia*, now with nearly a 45 degree list, was towed out of Larnaca harbour to avoid blocking it and the crew were taken off.

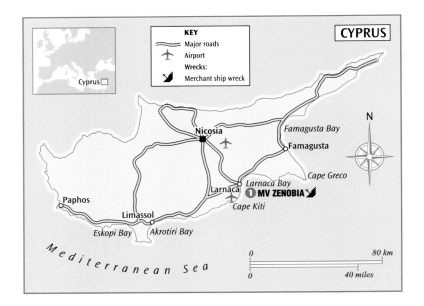

Loaded with over 100 trucks, trailers and other vehicles, industrial machinery and other cargo, she sank at 02:30 on Saturday 7 June, with more than £200 million worth of payload lost.

Easy to dive if you avoid deep penetration, the *Zenobia* now lies on her port side with her bows pointing south and her decks almost vertical in 43m (141ft) of water and rises to 16m (53ft). She is intact and carpeted in algae, while the bridge, restaurant and lifeboat deck are all accessible and can be visited without descending below 30m (98ft).

In many ways the *Zenobia* is like a civilian version of the *Thistlegorm* in Egypt's Red Sea (see page 89). Artefacts that can be seen include air-conditioning units, marble, glasses, cutlery, crockery, beer and Coca-Cola bottles, etc. The good visibility outside the vessel can easily lure inexperienced divers inside. If you do penetrate, you need a good light and a spare. The plasterboard partition walls have all collapsed and there is plenty of silt that can be disturbed to ruin the visibility and make it hard to find your way back out. So, unless you are a very experienced wreck diver, it is best to take a guided tour. The sheer size of the wreck is impressive.

Opposite: A diver hovering over one of the vehicles that were part of the cargo lost with the MV *Zenobia*.

Left: The huge anchor of the MV *Zenobia* is still in position.

RED SEA

EGYPT

By Jack Jackson

Separating two continents, the Red Sea is a long, narrow strip of water extending from the Gulf of Suez in the north-northwest to the Bab-el-Mandeb (gate of tears) in the south-southeast, where it joins the main Indian Ocean via the Gulf of Aden. Its extremely busy shipping lane is made even narrower by many coral reefs that rise steeply to the surface, and are difficult to see, so ships drifting off course often collide with them. In addition to navigational error and insurance fraud, there are many wrecks dating from World War II, when ships waiting to pass through the Suez Canal came within reach of German bombers based in the Mediterranean Sea. Boats of all sizes, legitimate or smuggling, have also come to grief while plying the sheltered Inner Passages. Thus divers have many wrecks to choose from, many of them in Egypt's waters.

Opposite: The SS *Thistlegorm* is every diver's dream because of its contents.

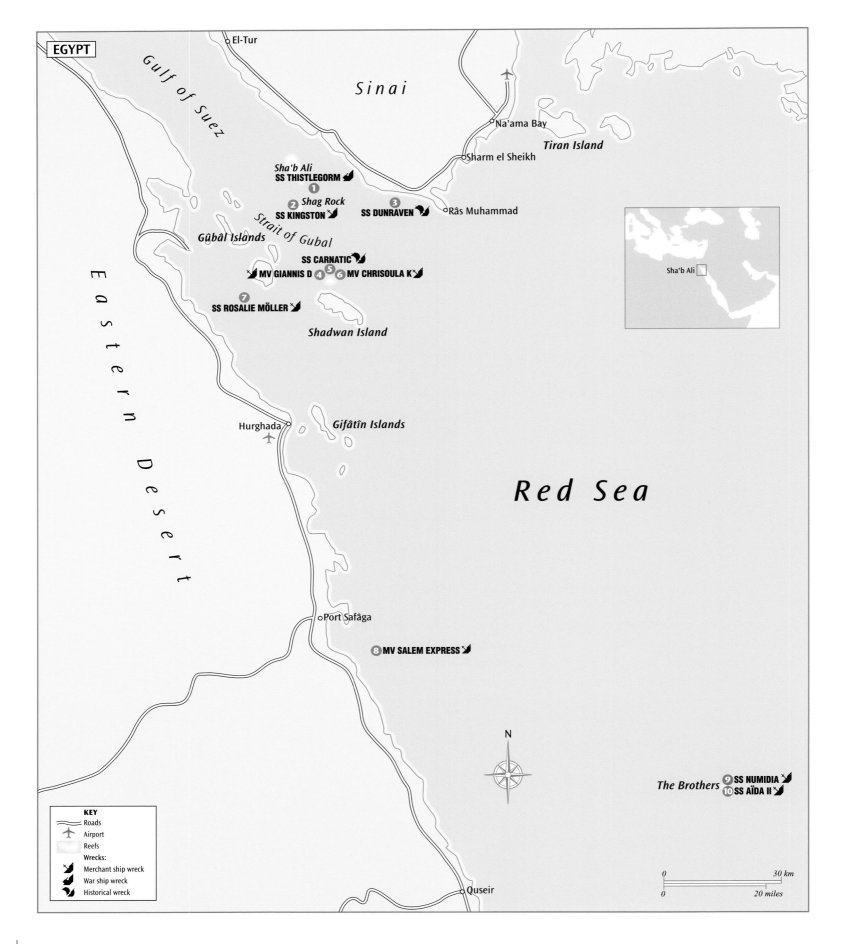

EGYPT

Gulf of Suez

El-Tur

Sinai

Na'ama Bay

Tiran Island

Sharm el Sheikh

Sha'b Ali
SS THISTLEGORM
❶

❷ *Shag Rock*
SS KINGSTON

❸ **SS DUNRAVEN**

Râs Muhammad

Gûbâl Islands

Strait of Gubal

Sha'b Ali

SS CARNATIC
✕ **MV GIANNIS D** ❹ ❺ ❻ **MV CHRISOULA K**

❼
SS ROSALIE MÖLLER

Shadwan Island

Eastern Desert

Hurghada

Gifâtîn Islands

Red Sea

Port Safâga

❽ **MV SALEM EXPRESS**

N

The Brothers ❾ **SS NUMIDIA**
❿ **SS AÏDA II**

KEY
— Roads
✈ Airport
▢ Reefs
Wrecks:
✕ Merchant ship wreck
✕ War ship wreck
✕ Historical wreck

0 ——————— 30 km
0 ——————— 20 miles

Quseir

The Red Sea is easy and cheap to reach from Europe and has good visibility, with warm water in summer and relatively warm water in winter, making it a popular destination. Wreck aficionados have found over 20 wrecks during the year 2005 alone. Egypt's first artificial reef, the *Hebat Allah*, was sunk near Hurghada between the popular sites of Gota Abu Ramada and El Aruk Giftûn with a maximum depth of 46m (151ft). In recent years, interest in mixed-gas technical diving has enabled divers to locate wrecks in deep water such as the *Jolanda/Yolanda* on Shark Reef at Egypt's Râs Muhammad and the SS *Maidan* off Rocky Islet.

SHA'B ALI AND SHAG ROCK

There are several wrecks around Sha'b Ali, including the *Carina*, the SS *Thistlegorm* and to the south, off Shag Rock, a Dornier bomber and, on its west side, the SS *Kingston*. Being close to the *Thistlegorm* the other wrecks are mostly ignored.

SS THISTLEGORM ❶

The 4,976 ton, 126.5m (415ft) *Thistlegorm* may not be the best wreck in the world, but it has become one of the most famous. She had a beam of 18m (59ft) and was the equivalent of a World War II army surplus store. Many who dive on the wreck act like children in a candy store and, being the most dived-on wreck in the world since its rediscovery in the early 1990s, diver traffic has taken its toll and many artefacts have now disappeared.

Powered by a triple-expansion, three-cylinder engine producing 365 horsepower, the *Thistlegorm* was one of a number of 'Thistle' ships owned and operated by the Albyn Line. She was built by JL Thompson and Sons at Sunderland in 1940. Requisitioned and armed by the Navy, she set off with supplies for the Western Desert (XIII) Force in North Africa. Because the Germans and Italians had control of most of the Mediterranean, she sailed the long way, around the Cape of Good Hope, and was

escorted up the Red Sea to Suez. Laden with military equipment – from trucks loaded with motorcycles, vehicle and aircraft parts, gun carriers, munitions and railway locomotives to radios and wellington boots – she was waiting with other ships at Sha'b Ali for clearance to enter the Suez Canal. Two vessels had collided further up the Gulf of Suez and were blocking the way. When two German Heinkel He-111 bombers from the 26th Kamp Geswader Squadron based in Crete failed to find their main target (a troopship), they bombed other ships instead. Early on 6 October 1941 two bombs hit the aft holds containing the ordnance of the *Thistlegorm*. The resulting explosions ripped a huge hole in the aft section and sent the two locomotives spiralling into the air as the ship was ripped open. The *Thistlegorm* was set on fire and soon sank. Four of the crew and five of the Royal Navy personnel on board to man the guns were killed. The survivors were rescued by HMS *Carlisle* but, as was the custom at the time, the surviving crew's pay was stopped and they had to make their own way home.

Poorly marked on the charts, the wreck remained undisturbed until the early fifties, when Jacques-Yves Cousteau's team on the *Calypso* found her. They raised several items from the wreck – including one of the motorcycles, the captain's safe and the ship's bell. They reported this in the February 1956 edition of *National Geographic* and the film and book *The Living Sea*. At that time amateur diving was not common in the Red Sea, so the *Thistlegorm* was forgotten until a British wreck fanatic began asking the right questions in the early 1990s. Local fishermen soon came up with the answer and the ship was rediscovered.

The dive is not quite as good as the Umbria in Sudan (see page 100), because the visibility is often poor and the currents are strong. In the early days it was possible to find tool kits under the seats of the motorcycles; Nurse Sharks and huge groupers rested among the wreckage, and the handrails were covered two crew, just two days after the *Thistlegorm*. Today the *Rosalie Möller* lies upright on sand with its starboard anchor running out. The bow is at 39m (128ft), the rudder at 45m (148ft) and the top of the mast at 17m (56ft). The cargo hatches and wooden deck have rotted away, revealing the cargo of coal. There are plenty of signs of salvage, but from a long while ago. One of the propeller blades is missing, but there are still some portholes. She should only be dived in the best weather, due to the currents and generally poor visibility. The fish and coral life is prolific, but because of the depth, divers' bottom time is limited.

SHA'B ABU NUHÂS

Just 3.6km (2½ miles) north of the western end of Shadwân Island (Shaker Island), Sha'b Abu Nuhâs is only visible at very low tides and is dangerously close to the shipping lane. Several ships have gone down here over the years, giving the best grouping on a single reef anywhere. Some of the wrecks are the result of navigational error or bad weather, but others appear to be insurance frauds because their listed cargo is missing. Along the northwest face, the *Giannis D* is near the western corner, the *Carnatic* is near the centre. Near the eastern corner, the *Chrisoula K* is next to earlier wrecks. In contrast to the other wrecks here, the *Carnatic* has over 100 years of coral growth. Some of the wrecks were named after their obvious cargo until they were properly identified.

MV GIANNIS D ❹

Built as the *Shoyo Maru* in Japan by the Kuryshima Dock Company of Imabari in 1969, the 2,932 ton freighter was sold to a Greek company in 1975 and renamed Markos. She was sold again in the early 1980s and renamed *Giannis D*, the large 'D' on the funnel refers to the Dumarc Shipping and Trading Corporation of Piraeus. With a length of 99.5m (326ft) and beam of 16m (52ft), she had a six-

cylinder diesel engine that produced 3,000 brake horsepower.

Heading south from Suez loaded with softwood for Saudi Arabia and Yemen, the *Giannis D* was at cruising speed when in the early hours of 19 April 1983 she suddenly veered off course and into the northwest corner of Sha'b Abu Nuhâs. The crew were rescued by an Egyptian tug to a Santa Fe platform. At 04:00 hours, divers on the nearby British live-aboard *Lady Jenny 3* heard the commotion over the radio and were soon able to inspect the abandoned vessel, which remained at the surface for six weeks before breaking into two and settling on the seabed.

Lying mostly in shallow water, the *Giannis D* is more or less along the reef in three sections, with the bow section towards the *Carnatic*. The wreck is broken at the centre, with the bow section lying on its port side at 18m (59ft). The front central section behind the bow is badly broken up. The stern section is relatively intact, but listing 45 degrees to port. The bridge, engine room and companionways here are easily accessible and not completely dark, but an underwater light is preferable. There are plenty of fish, including the ubiquitous glassfish, scorpionfish and lionfish, and young soft and stony corals. With depths of only 4m (13ft) to the mast and 27m (89ft) to the seabed at the stern, there is plenty of light to add to the framing of the structure to produce good atmospheric photographs. Most divers will head straight for the stern, but the *Giannis D* is a great dive for divers of every level of experience.

SS CARNATIC ❺

The Peninsula & Oriental Passenger/Mail Steamer *Carnatic* was a steam-assisted square-rigged sailing vessel of 1,776 tons built by Samuda Brothers of Poplar, London in 1862. She had a primitive four-cylinder inverted compound engine producing 2,442 horsepower at a time when such ships could travel faster under sail if there was a good wind. The 90m

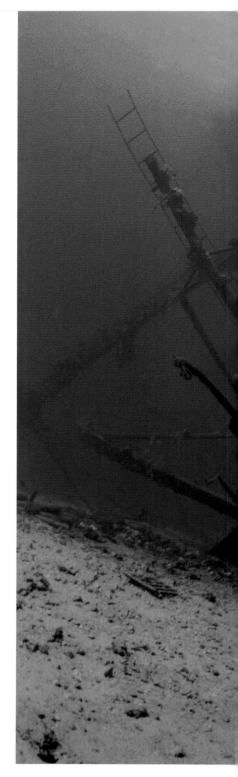

Above: The wreck of the MV *Giannis D* is shallow enough for divers to obtain atmospheric photographs.

(295ft) iron-frame vessel had a beam of 11.6m (38ft) and could carry 250 passengers.

During 1869 the Suez Canal was only just nearing completion and passengers and cargo travelled overland between Alexandria and Suez. On 12 September 1869 the *Carnatic* left Suez for Bombay with 230 passengers and crew in addition to a cargo of cotton bales, copper sheeting, Royal Mail, and £40,000 in specie and bullion. At 01:00 on 13 September, she struck Sha'b Abu Nuhâs and sprang a leak. At first it was thought that the ship's pumps were coping and some of the cotton was offloaded to reduce the weight, but eventually the boiler room flooded and the ship lost all power. On the morning of 14 September the order was finally given to abandon ship. However, while this was being done, the *Carnatic* suddenly split into two, the aft section sinking with 26 passengers and crew. The forward section fell to port and slipped off the reef, spilling more passengers and crew into the water. A total of 27 people drowned.

The lifeboats made their way across the reefs to Shadwân, where the survivors set fire to bales of cotton as a beacon because they knew that another P&O Liner – the *Sumatra*, inbound for Suez – was due to pass by at any time. All the survivors were rescued by the *Sumatra*.

The mail and bullion were of great value, so Lloyd's immediately set up a salvage operation with the only diver available. One body was recovered, mail bags were sent to the surface, valuables removed from the safe and the boxes of bullion recovered. Local Bedouin free divers recovered over 700 sheets of fine-grade copper destined for India's Mint by diving down and attaching ropes to them.

Lying roughly in the centre of the north face, the *Carnatic* was rediscovered by the crew members of the *Lady Jenny V* live-aboard in May 1984 while they were looking for another wreck. Lying parallel with the reef, the vessel is on her port side with the bows facing east, the stern facing west and the keel towards the reef. Surprisingly, the two halves of the ship have fallen to the seabed just as they might have done had they gone down as one piece. The fore and aft sections are still relatively intact, but the section between them is very badly damaged. The stern is on sand at 24m (79ft) and the bow at 18m (59ft) and the highest point 15m (49ft).

The wooden superstructure and deck have rotted away, leaving the iron framework of the vessel's three decks, so penetration is easy. The stern is photogenic inside and out, but so is the whole vessel. Having been underwater for over 100 years, the stony and soft coral growth is very good. There is prolific fish life, including a large shoal of sweepers (glassfish). It

is best for divers to ascend the reef slowly back into shallow water.

MV CHRISOULA K ⑥

The 3,720 tonne Greek freighter MV *Chrisoula K* struck the eastern approaches to the northern end of Sha'b Abu Nuhâs in 1981. She had a length of 98m (322ft) and a beam of 15m (49ft), and was powered by a 9-cylinder diesel engine giving 2,700 brake horsepower. She was built by Orenstein, Koppel and Luebekker in Lubeck, Germany, and launched in 1954 as the *Dora Oldendorf*. In 1970 she was renamed *Anna B* by new owners, and in 1979 she was bought by the Clarion Marine Company of Piraeus, Greece and renamed *Chrisoula K*.

Carrying Italian floor tiles bound for Jeddah, Saudi Arabia, the *Chrisoula K* drove hard into the reef on 31 August 1981. Rescue units from an Egyptian naval base picked up the crew and no lives were lost. The bow and foremast used to be obvious markers of this otherwise treacherous reef, but the Egyptian authorities deemed them to be a navigational hazard and removed them. This caused considerable damage to the fore section, which was eventually pounded to pieces by the waves and now rises to about 4m (13ft).

The main body of the *Chrisoula K* is generally upright; it slopes down the reef crest and lies on sand with the stern separating and listing well to starboard from around 27m (89ft). The wide cargo holds are easily penetrated, but penetration of the closed-in parts of the ship including the engine room inside the stern is only recommended to divers who are well trained in wreck penetration. There are the ubiquitous shoals of glassfish (sweepers).

The *Chrisoula K* is now colonized by stony and soft corals and harbours many species of reef fish. The reef in this area is relatively sheltered and many parts are of a vertical profile, making for a good dive. Together with the wreck there are a variety of different dives to cater for all levels of diving

experience. Wreckage from the other ships that have foundered on the same corner of the reef (including the *Kimon M*) can be found strewn all over this section of Sha'b Abu Nuhâs.

MV SALEM EXPRESS ❽
On 15 December 1991 the 4,771 tonne roll-on roll-off ferry, the *Salem Express*, was en route from Jeddah to Port Safâga crammed with Muslim pilgrims returning from Mecca on the Hajj. She was travelling nearer the Egyptian coast than usual for protection from a gale when, close to midnight, she hit the southern end of a chain of reefs known as Hyndman Reefs. The vessel's special pivoting loading doors burst open, flooding the vehicle deck. She sank too quickly for the crew to release the lifeboats or to

give out a mayday call, and the alarm was only raised when a survivor managed to swim to the mainland. The official passenger list was less than 700 and the official death toll under 470, but in fact she was heavily overcrowded and it is thought that the real figures were considerably higher. Surprisingly, 180 people survived, with most of them managing to swim ashore.

Many bodies were recovered from the accommodation along the upper port side, but deeper penetration became too dangerous, so the Egyptian Navy sealed the vessel from further intrusion.

Built in the French shipyard of Constructions Navales et Industrielles de la Meditérranée at La Seyne in 1964, the ship was launched as the *Fred*

Left: A diver looking over the stern of the SS *Carnatic*, which is encrusted with marine organisms.

Scamaroni. During later years, the vessel's owners and name were changed several times until, in 1988, she finally became the *Salem Express*. She had a length of 100m (328ft) and a beam of 18m (59ft) and was powered by four diesel engines producing 14,880 brake horsepower of thrust in different directions. Being a roll-on roll-off ferry, her bow had a lifting mechanism designed to pivot the entire forward bow upwards. This mechanism played an important part in her sinking.

The *Salem Express* is the most controversial wreck dive in the Red Sea due to the tragic loss of life when she sank. An eerie wreck, because of the way she is lit, the *Salem Express* now lies completely on her starboard side in 30m (98ft) of water with her port side at 12m (39ft). The authorities have sealed the interior because of human remains, but there are personal effects scattered everywhere. Lifeboats still

hang from their davits, soft corals colonize the funnels and frogfish are common. Apart from her bow doors being forced open, she looks as though she is sailing on her side and has the proud insignia 'S' on the funnels. Because of the way she is lying, the wreck is better lit in the morning.

THE BROTHERS
SS NUMIDIA ❾

The Brothers (El Akhawein), 52km (32 miles) east-northeast of El Quseir, are two isolated islands rising out of deep water. Big Brother has a lighthouse at the centre of the southwest face and is only about 400m (1,312ft) long, but it dwarfs Little Brother a kilometre to the southeast. Part of the Offshore Marine Park Islands, with strong currents promoting the growth of a spectacular Dendronephthya Soft Tree Corals, Big Brother has two wrecks at its

Left: Coral-encrusted rolling stock used to be the signature picture of the SS *Numidia*, but some disappeared in the summer of 2006.

northern tip. The SS *Numidia*, which sank in 1901, lies very steeply down the northernmost tip, starting at 9m (30ft) with the stern at 80m (262ft). About 100m (328ft) south of the *Numidia* is the wreck of the SS *Aïda*, which sank in 1957. The bow section is unrecognizable, but the stern lies at 30–65m (98–213ft) and the rest is scattered over the reef.

The 6,399 ton British freighter *Numidia* was built in Glasgow by D&W Henderson in 1901 and operated by the Anchor Line at the time of her loss. She was 137.4m (451ft) long, with a beam of 16.7m (55ft) and was powered by a three-cylinder triple expansion steam engine that gave her a top speed of 10 knots.

At about two in the morning of 20 July 1901 she ran aground on Big Brother Island where, although she was stuck fast, she remained afloat for some weeks. This allowed salvage, and no lives were lost.

Though seemingly at an impossible angle and plunging into technical diving depths, this is a most beautiful wreck due to the soft corals. Ideally divers should aim for the least current, but some current is required to show the Dendronephthya Soft Tree Corals at their best. Divers can shelter from the currents within the superstructure. Visitors have not been able to take many artefacts, so the outline of the metal parts of the ship is still well marked, the lifeboat davits and winches are all still in place and the resident marine life includes big groupers. The coral-encrusted rolling stock wheels, the signature image of the *Numidia*, disappeared in the summer of 2006.

SS AÏDA ⑩

The 1,428 tonne SS *Aïda* was built in France in 1911. She was 75.1m (246ft) long, with a 9.7m (32ft) beam, and was powered by a single three-cylinder triple expansion engine giving a top speed of 9 knots. Bought for the Egyptian Ports and Lighthouses Administration, she was later used to ferry troops. Damaged in a World War II air raid, she was

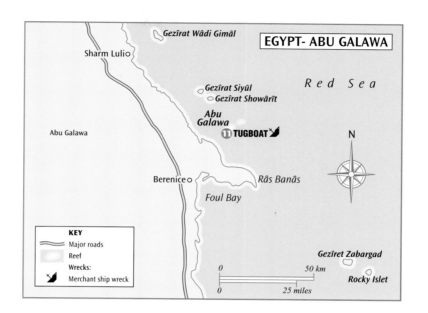

repaired and reused and this is possibly where the term Aïda II came from.

On 15 September 1957, while attempting to change the troops on Big Brother Island in a storm, the *Aïda* struck rocks and began to sink. A single dive is not adequate to cover both wrecks at The Brothers.

ABU GALAWA
TUGBOAT ⑪

Abu Galawa has the wreck of a tugboat, thought to be the MV *Tienstin*, 17km (10½ miles) north-northwest of Râs Banâs. She is leaning on the western end of the south side of the reef and listing to starboard. The bow of the wreck lies on the reef and breaks the surface, while the stern is on sand at 18m (59ft). Artefacts found on the wreck appear to date from the 1950s, but the growth of stony coral is phenomenal. The holds and Western-style toilet harbour shoals of glassfish (sweepers); the propeller is still attached; and the hull has a prolific growth of stony and soft coral, including some large Porites. This is a very easy dive, including penetration.

SUDAN

By Jack Jackson

Although currently difficult to reach due to unreliable flights, Sudanese waters north of Port Sudan have the best diving and largest species diversity in all of the Red Sea. Sudan has the deepest and warmest waters found anywhere, with depths reaching 3,000m (9,800ft) between Port Sudan and Jeddah. Isolated coral atolls and pinnacles rise vertically from very deep water to touch the surface, giving great diving among prolific marine life, healthy corals, brilliant visibility and large fish. There are so many shallow reefs that are not visible before 10:00 hours, after 16:00 hours or on cloudy days that ships regularly come to grief on them.

Opposite: The cab of a Toyota truck that fell off from the deck of the *Blue Belt* when she was pulled over by tugs.

MV BLUE BELT ❶

Sailing from Jeddah, Saudi Arabia, to Port Sudan, the *Blue Belt* was well off route for large ships when she went aground on Sha'b Su'adi on 2 December 1977. Two tugs from Port Sudan tried to pull her off, but too enthusiastically – and she overturned, sinking on 5 December 80km (50 miles) north of Port Sudan.

The *Blue Belt* was a 2,399 ton freighter, with a length of 103.8m (341ft) and a 14m (46ft) beam, originally built in the Howaldts-Werke A.G. shipyard for the Hamburg Amerika line in 1950. She was named Hamburg and registered in Hamburg. In 1953 she was renamed *Coburg*. In 1971 she was sold to Navegadora Panoceania SA, who registered her in Panama and renamed her *Green Belt*. In 1972 she was sold to Ahmed Mohamed Baaboud and Ahmed Mohamed Baghlaf, who reregistered her in Saudi Arabia and renamed her *Blue Belt*. At the time of her sinking, the *Blue Belt* was carrying cars, trucks, tractors and spares, mostly Toyotas, and local dive operators now refer to her as the Toyota wreck.

The wreck is upside down with the top of the bow at 20m (66ft) and the rest of the ship dropping down the reef at an angle of 50 degrees on a steep drop-off. The stern lies at about 83m (272ft). Getting into the ship can be an awkward dive due to it being upside down, so divers have to descend again to the depth of their entry point at the end of the dive.

Some of the vehicles carried as deck cargo spilled off onto the sand at 15m (49ft) when the ship overturned and these make an interesting dive, remarkable for the sponge growth.

CONSHELF II ❷

Sha'b Rumi (Roman Reef) lies east of Marsa 'Arus, 40km (25 miles) north-northeast of Port Sudan. The west side of the reef has two entrances to its lagoon. Just outside the southern entrance, lying on a ledge at 9m (30ft), are the remains of Jacques-Yves Cousteau's 1963 *Conshelf II* experiment. The largest of the remains is the onion-shaped submersible hangar. Its

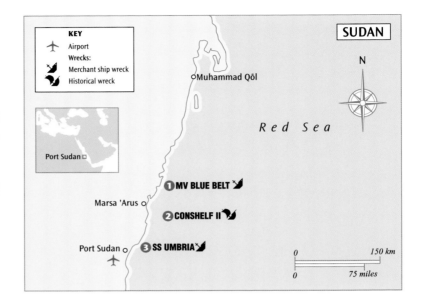

portholes have gone, but the roof holds an air pocket of divers' exhaust gases. East of the hanger lie cables that ran to the utility ship *Rosaldo* in the lagoon, and just to the north of the hangar is the tool shed. Further north, abreast of the lagoon entrance, three multicoloured fish pens covered in Dendronephthya Soft Tree Corals move around in rough seas. Over the drop-off a shark cage is the only remnant of the deep habitat at 27m (89ft).

Inconsiderate divers have broken off some of the table corals on the hangar, but the site is still full of nostalgia and makes an excellent night dive. The memorial casket under the submarine hangar is inscribed to a German diver who died on the reef in 1973. The best time to dive the site is very early morning.

SS UMBRIA ❸

If ever a wreck was designed to please recreational divers, it is the *Umbria*. Scuttled in shallow water and sheltered by Wingate reefs she can be dived in any weather. There is no current, lots of light, great visibility, abundant coral growth and prolific marine life.

Originally named *Bahia Blanca*, this 10,076 ton, 155m (508ft) combined cargo and passenger vessel,

with a beam of 18m (59ft), was powered by triple-expansion six-cylinder engines producing 848 nominal horsepower. She was built in Hamburg by Reihersts Shiffswerke in 1912. Before World War II she was sold to Lloyd Triestino Di Navigazione Societa Per Azioni, renamed *Umbria* and registered at Genoa. On 12 June 1940 she was anchored outside Port Sudan harbour when Italy entered the war in support of Germany. Knowing that it carried munitions, vehicle and aircraft spares hidden under cement and foodstuffs, the British Authorities seized the ship. However, the crew had opened the seacocks and the captain lied about timed fuses, which he said had been set in the munitions holds, and the ship was abandoned to sink.

In 1949, against local thinking that the sharks would attack him, Hans Hass became the first civilian to dive on the *Umbria*. It was his book *Under the Red Sea*, first published in 1952, and his subsequent films that attracted the world's top underwater photographers to the site.

Today the *Umbria* lies at an angle on her port side, with her starboard davits breaking the surface. The port propeller is buried in the coral, but the starboard propeller is in clear water at 15m (49ft). The stern rests on coral at 20m (66ft), while the bow rests on sand at 36m (118ft). Penetrating most of the ship is easy. The gangways are clear and the holds are open. Munitions, aircraft and vehicle parts, wine bottles, batteries and Kilner jars are scattered around. A hold in front of the wheelhouse contains three Fiat 1100 Lunga cars. Many sacks are no longer supported so divers require good buoyancy control to avoid dislodging them. Entering the engine room and kitchen are more difficult; divers must be careful not to disturb the silt, or they will not be able to see their way out again. A fixed safety guideline is a prudent precaution here. The engines are still intact and an outboard motor is still clamped to the engine room wall. The *Umbria* is one of the world's greatest dives.

Above left: The *Umbria* can be seen from above and its starboard davits break the surface.

Above right: The visibility on *Umbria* is so good that all of the stern can be photographed without the addition of flash.

INDIAN OCEAN

AUSTRALIA – West Coast

By Rochelle Mutton

WRECKS FEATURED
★HMAS SWAN
★HMAS PERTH

In its northern part Australia's west coast diving is best known for Ningaloo Reef's whale shark migration to feed on plankton when the corals spawn, manta rays, tiger sharks and the islands and shoals further north. At the southern end there is more excellent and popular diving, whales, whale-watching and many wrecks, some of which were purposely sunk for divers. There are marine parks close to Perth and an unusual heritage trail for snorkellers, the Rottnest Heritage Trail, with wrecks dating back to the 1880s. Preparing Australia's first artificial wreck, the HMAS *Swan*, was a huge undertaking and those concerned took advice from the experts, the Artificial Reef Society in British Columbia, Canada. When the larger HMAS *Perth* was sunk more of her original fittings were left, including gun turrets, control panels and furniture.

Opposite: Longfin Spadefish (*Platax tiera*), also known as Longfin Batfish, at the HMAS *Swan* wreck off Dunsborough in southwest Western Australia.

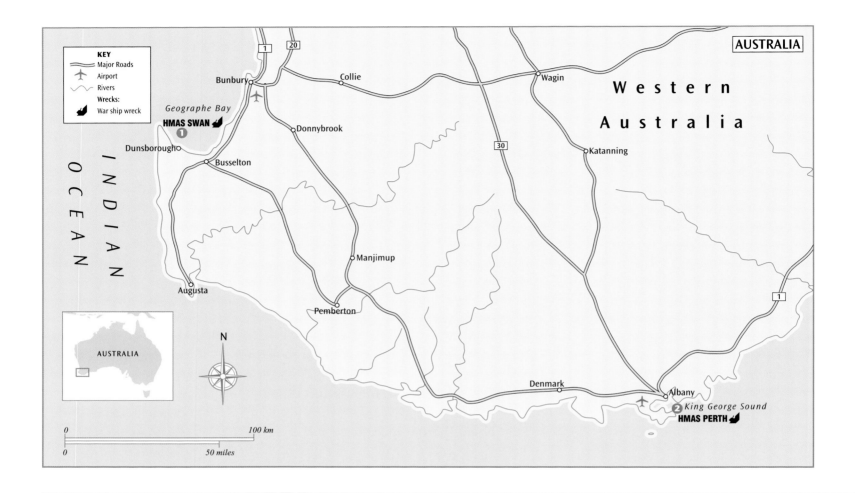

KEY
~ Major Roads
✈ Airport
~ Rivers
Wrecks:
War ship wreck

AUSTRALIA

1
20
Bunbury
Collie
Wagin
Geographe Bay
HMAS SWAN ❶
Dunsborough
Busselton
Donnybrook
30
Katanning
Western Australia
INDIAN OCEAN
Manjimup
Augusta
Pemberton
AUSTRALIA
N
Denmark
Albany
King George Sound
HMAS PERTH ❷
1
0   100 km
0   50 miles

HMAS SWAN ❶

In one of Western Australia's picture-postcard bays lies a hulking sea warrior that was purposely sunk as the ideal dive wreck. Descending the mooring rope, the wreck of the former HMAS *Swan* appears at first as a ghostly shadow, then materializes into a naval giant. From its underwater grave, the ship is experiencing a second life that can be explored by beginner, advanced and specialized penetration divers alike.

The wreck of the *Swan* lies in Geographe Bay, near the holiday town of Dunsborough, 255km (158 miles) south of Perth, capital of Western Australia. Guided tours are available from the sole commercial dive operator, which launches its rigid inflatable from the sandy beach. It takes about 15 minutes to reach the wreck site. Dolphins often frolic alongside the charter boat. The bay is also the regular haunt of Humpback Whales that have discovered that the wreck is useful as a giant back-scratcher. The ship's side carries the scars of contact left by whales scraping barnacles from their skin. A 'no fishing' sign and red buoys are the only topside markers for the ship's position. The two buoys, more than 100m (328ft) apart, denote the ship's bow and stern and promise a wreck of impressive proportions.

The *Swan* was the most expensive and complex warship of her time, costing the Australian Navy $22m to build. Launched in 1970 with great fanfare at the Naval Dockyards in Williamston, Victoria, the vessel was struck with a champagne bottle 11 times before finally being christened and released down the slipway. Designated as a 'River' Class Destroyer Escort, the *Swan* was named after the river that runs through Perth. Commissioned as HMAS *Swan*, but affectionately known as Fluffy Duck, the ship carried a crew of 250 and was fitted with the latest technology, including a computer-controlled and radar-guided gun turret. However, the actual ship's frame was an old design.

During her 26 years of service, HMAS *Swan* travelled 1,481,600km (800,000 nautical miles) and served during the Vietnam War (although she saw no action). After being decommissioned, the *Swan* was given by the Australian Commonwealth Government to the State of Western Australia, which invited communities to make submissions on her future use. Ideas such as a floating museum, floating restaurant, floating church and homeless shelter were considered. It was finally decided to sink her as a dive wreck 2.4km (1½ nautical miles) off the coast of Point Piquet, Meelup Beach. Hundreds of volunteers

Below: A diver hovering by the communication tower of the HMAS *Swan*, which has various antennae.

took part in the painstaking stripping and cleaning of the ship's interior, removing many kilometres of cabling, as well as 7,000 litres (1,540 gallons) of oil, plastics and hydraulic fluid. The engine and boiler rooms were sealed off for diver safety. On 13 September 1996 the *Swan* was christened as an artificial reef – the first ship to be prepared as a dive wreck in the Southern Hemisphere. A raffle granted the honour of detonating the explosives to a man who passed it onto his six-year-old son.

The 113m (371ft) warship has a beam of 12.5m (41ft), and is peppered with giant holes that give its marine inhabitants and visiting divers plenty of easy entries and exits. Standing upright at 23m (75ft) from top to bottom, the *Swan* hosts several ecosystem tiers and has attracted about 80 fish species since it was sunk. Perfect for shallow dives and safety stops, the uppermost crow's nest supports the greatest amount of growth. Residential Teira Batfish hover in the sunlight and the railings, plastered in bright Telesto soft corals, have little blennies popping out at intervals from the hollow ends. Across the coral-encrusted deck flash dozens of impressive Samson Fish, on the hunt for tasty morsels. Taut, as if standing to attention, are Sergeant Bakers with a long dorsal filament, while other fish flit gently across the silty deck, including Moonlighters, Old Wives and Magpie Perch. Inside the hull, hundreds of little bullseyes hover in the eerie still of ship's cabins. Here there are plenty of colourful fish such as the spectacularly bright Blue Devil, dainty cowfish with swirling patterns and various wrasse species. Protected by the vicinity's 200m (220 yard) fishing ban, large blue groupers reside undisturbed in the hold.

The room most popular with divers is the bridge, where the captain's chair has an eerie, elevated view through a line of square, open windows, onto the deck below. Directly below, the operations room displays the shells of switch panels, and in the middle is an old radar station with faded compass bearings. Two funnel uptakes, located above the boiler room,

offer divers a swim-through with a difference as they rise up through three deck-levels. The ship's rooms have all sorts of remains from the days of active service, including basins and toilets. The bow rests on the sandy seabed at 30m (98ft), forming a cave where wobbegongs rest by the rudders.

HMAS PERTH ❷

The *Swan* is the best known of the trail of dive wrecks along the Western Australian coast, but another deliberately sunk decommissioned warship, the HMAS *Perth*, is also gaining popularity.

There have been three Australian Navy vessels called HMAS *Perth*. This second HMAS *Perth* (D-38/38) was a Charles F. Adams-class guided missile destroyer, laid down by Defoe Shipbuilding Company at Bay City, Michigan, USA on 21 September 1962. She was launched on 26 September 1963 and commissioned on 17 July 1965. The HMAS *Perth* served as plane guard for carriers on Yankee Station in the Tonkin Gulf and took part in Operation Sea Dragon and Operation Market Time. She carried out search and rescue duties and Naval Gunfire Support missions during the conflict in Vietnam. HMAS *Perth* was awarded the United States Navy Unit Commendation and Meritorious Unit Commendation for her service in Vietnam.

The Charles F. Adams class of guided missile destroyers was a group of 29 built between 1958 and 1967. Twenty-three of these ships were built for the United States Navy, three for the Royal Australian Navy, and three for the West German Navy. The ships were based on the existing Forrest Sherman class, but were the first destroyers designed to serve as missile destroyers.

Located in a bay famous for whales – once hunted, now an ecotourism drawcard – the former HMAS *Perth* was the biggest warship to be made into a dive wreck at the time when it was sunk in King George Sound, on 24 November 2001. The *Perth* lies off the southern coast at Albany, some

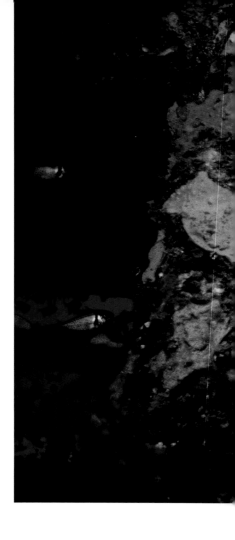

409km (254 miles) from its capital city namesake. The former guided missile destroyer had a distinguished 34-year service record and has been the only Australian ship hit by enemy fire, when she was scarred by an artillery shell fired on 18 October 1967 during the Vietnam conflict. Despite its long, narrow hull – 133m (436ft) in length – and a top-heavy frame that made it prone to listing, the *Perth* was expertly sunk with explosives into an upright position. The topmast protrudes from the water surface, offering shallow dives and interesting safety stops, including a platform at 5m (16ft).

This HMAS *Perth* took part in three tours in Vietnam: 2 September 1967 to 10 April 1968; 14 September 1968 to 20 April 1969; 14 September 1970 to 8 April 1971. On her first tour, on 18 October 1967, she was hit by an artillery shell which penetrated one deck. In her six-month deployment the HMAS *Perth* came under fire four times.

The wreck has six moorings, four for lease strictly to commercial dive charters and the other two strictly reserved for public use on a first-come, first-served basis, with a two-hour limit. Boats cannot drop anchor, and a 250-m (820-ft) diameter fishing exclusion zone is in force around the wreck. An interpretive dive trail in the upper superstructure is marked by a series of plaques with information on marine flora and fauna, including sponges, anemones, a pictorial fish guide, mussels, oysters, scallops and sea squirts (ascidians). Proper training and equipment is mandatory before attempting penetration, but holes cut into the ship are especially designed for safe scuba-diving. Attached to a beam is an underwater camera that can be viewed via live streaming on the Internet. Located in an area frequented by Samson and kingfish, it has given rise to cyber 'fishing' competitions, in which web visitors can capture images of passing fish, and submit their 'catch' to the judges. A second dive trail is planned that will tell the history of the *Perth*.

PACIFIC OCEAN

MALAYSIA

By Jack Jackson

Because of its links with ancient trade routes there are a considerable number of wrecks in Malaysian waters, including those that carried valuable ancient Chinese ceramics. However, because of the depths involved, most of these have been salvaged commercially. Many of the wrecks from more recent times are very deep; and recreational technical divers are now taking an interest in them for treasure. However, normal recreational divers are more interested in vessels that sank in World War II, or later, in shallower water.

Opposite: The Cement Wreck *Tung Hwang* is covered in a remarkable amount of marine growth.

The vessels regularly dived in Peninsular Malaysia include the 32,000 ton battle cruiser HMS *Repulse* and the 35,000 ton battleship HMS *Prince of Wales* off Kuantan. Both are protected as British war graves, from World War II, which means look-but-do-not-touch. More recent wrecks include the 98,000 ton Swedish tanker *Seven Skies* further to the south. In East Malaysia divers can now get to the World War II wrecks in the Balabac Strait, which separates Palawan and Malaysian Borneo, and to those around the Mantanani Islands and Usukan Bay. Two American submarines, the USS *Darter* and the USS *Dace*, caused havoc among Japanese shipping here at the end of World War II. There are also wrecks off Labuan and Sarawak, with the ones off Labuan being the most frequently dived of all the wrecks in Malaysia. At the northern mouth of Brunei Bay, 8km (5 miles) off mainland Sabah, 115km (71 miles) south of Kota Kinabalu, Pulau Labuan's reefs have four good shipwrecks. All the wrecks experience strong surface currents, but divers can quickly descend to the leeward sides of the wrecks.

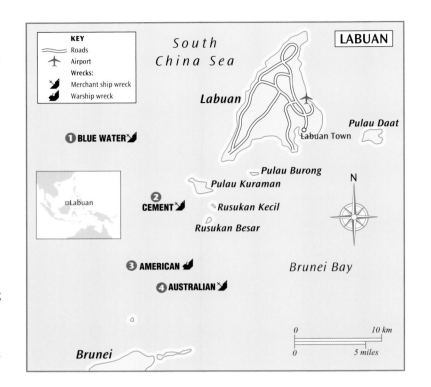

BLUE WATER WRECK ❶

The Blue Water Wreck is the Philippine stern trawler MV *Mabini Padre*, 30km (20 miles) directly west of the Labuan marina, northwest of Kuraman Island. She caught fire and sank on 13 November 1981 while in tow. The 1,654 ton trawler, with a length of 80m (262ft) and a 12m (39ft) beam, is now lying on her port side at 35m (115ft) with the starboard side at 24m (79ft). She gets her nickname from the clear, blue water around her. She is still completely intact; the fish life is quite good, but the coral is poor.

CEMENT WRECK ❷

The Cement Wreck 20km (12½ miles) south-southwest of the Labuan Marina, is the 2,697 ton Japanese freighter *Tung Hwang* that was discovered on 25 September 1980. She was carrying cement when she went down. This had been intended for the new palace of the Sultan of Brunei, but it had been rejected as inferior quality. She has a length of 92m (302ft) and a 15m (49ft) beam. Easy to penetrate, the freighter lies upright on the bottom at 30m (98ft), with some broken masts rising to 8m (26ft). The main deck is at 19m (62ft). This wreck has colourful soft corals, sponges and feather stars covering the superstructure, and the fish life is prolific. The visibility is usually better than on the other Labuan wrecks, but divers should be careful of several fishing nets that have snagged on it. This is the best of the Labuan wrecks for underwater photography.

AMERICAN WRECK ❸

The American Wreck, 24km (15 miles) southwest of Labuan Marina, southwest of the island of Rusukan Besar, has been identified as the US Navy Admirable Class mine hunter, USS *Salute*, which was sunk by a Japanese mine on 17 June 1945 during the Allies' pre-invasion sweep of Brunei Bay – Operation Oboe

Six. The *Salute* and other vessels of Mine Division 34 were sweeping the approaches, clearing a path for troop landings on Labuan and Brunei. She hit a mine at 15:15 and sank. Four men died in the blast and 37 were wounded. The 800 ton *Salute* was 56m (184ft) long and with a 10m (33ft) beam. She was laid down on 11 November 1942 by Winslow Marine Railway and Shipbuilding Co. of Seattle, Washington, USA. Launched on 6 February 1943 and sponsored by Miss Patricia Lindgren, she was commissioned on 4 December 1943.

The wreck now lies at 30m (98ft), broken in half and folded back on itself with the bow lying on top of the stern. The shallowest part of the wreck, the bow, rises to 12m (39ft).

AUSTRALIAN WRECK ❹
The Australian Wreck 23km (14 miles) southwest of Labuan Marina, southwest of the island of Rusukan Besar, has now been identified as the 2,071 ton Dutch passenger/freighter SS *De Klerk*. She was 90m (279ft) long and had a beam of 12m (39ft). There are conflicting reports as to whether she was built in Britain around 1890 or in Amsterdam in 1900. She was taken over by the Dutch Indies Government at the end of January 1942 for conversion to a troop carrier for the Royal Dutch Navy at Tjilatjap. The conversion was cancelled due to a shortage of personnel, and the Navy scuttled her on 2 March 1942 at Tandjong Priok, Java, to prevent the vessel from falling into Japanese hands. However, the Japanese salvaged the ship on 28 November 1942 and added it to the Japanese fleet as the Imbari Maru.

The vessel left Sarawak on 15 September 1944 for Manila with 1,210 people on board. She was either bombed or hit a mine, and sank on the 16th, with the loss of 308 'workers', 26 'comfort women' and 5 Japanese soldiers.

She now lies at a 50-degree angle on her port side, on sand at 33m (69ft). The davits reach 18m (59ft).

Below: Dendronephthya Soft Tree corals among other soft corals on a grid by the funnel of the Cement Wreck *Tung Hwang*.

PHILIPPINES

By Jack Jackson

Wrecks in the Philippines include the remains of galleons that carried rich cargoes, and junks that carried valuable ceramics. Most of these have been either salvaged commercially or pirated by local people. However, recreational divers are more interested in the more modern vessels, most of which were sunk in World War II. These vessels include those found at Subic Bay; several Japanese ships found around Busuanga and Coron Islands in the Calamian Group; and two located at Pearl Farm, Davao, Mindanao Island.

Opposite: The sponge-covered superstructure provides a hiding place for fish on the wreck of the Japanese provision ship *Irako*, Coron.

SUBIC BAY

EX-USS NEW YORK ❶

The withdrawal of US Forces from the Philippines in November 1992 was a bonus for divers. During the American administration, civilian diving was prohibited on the wrecks in Subic Bay, and naval personnel after 1978. Now these wrecks are available to recreational divers. The Bay is policed to stop people stealing artefacts from the wrecks, and dive operators require permits for divers. The most significant wreck here is the old Armoured Cruiser ex-USS *New York*. Authorized by Congress in 1888, she was built by the Philadelphia shipyard of William Cramp and Sons. She was launched on 2 December 1891 and commissioned on 1 August 1893. The 8,150 ton vessel was 116m (380ft 6in) long, with a beam of 19.8m (64ft 10in). Her four triple-expansion engines generated 17,401 horsepower, giving a top speed of 21 knots.

For armament she carried eighteen guns in her main battery, made up of twelve 10cm (4in) and six 20cm (8in) guns, various smaller guns and torpedo tubes of 35.6cm (14in). Her armour varied from 7.6cm (3in) to 25.4cm (10in) thick.

The USS *New York*'s first assignment was with the South Atlantic Squadron from January to March 1894. She was transferred to the North Atlantic Squadron in August that year and to the European Squadron in 1895. In 1897 she was serving as flagship of the North Atlantic Squadron when, under Rear Admiral William T. Sampson, she took part in the Spanish-American war.

On 14 August 1898 she was received with great celebration in New York, after which she was moved around the world. In 1899 she served around South America and was the first of three US naval units to be fitted with wireless. In 1901 she sailed to Cavite, Philippines, to become the flagship of the Asiatic Fleet, seeing service in the Philippines-American war and the Chinese revolution, and returning to the

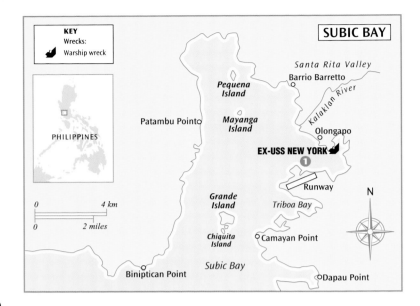

United States in 1902. By 1903 she was serving in the Pacific Squadron, becoming its flagship in 1904.

Decommissioned for overhaul in January 1905, the USS *New York* was recommissioned in 1909 and served in the Mediterranean before being placed on reserve. In 1910 she sailed for Manila to rejoin the Asiatic Squadron, and in 1911 she gave up the name *New York* to the US Navy's new battleship and was renamed USS *Saratoga*. She returned to the United States in 1916 and was put on reserve again.

She was recommissioned for World War I as part of Pacific Patrol Force 7. In 1917 she took a third name, USS *Rochester*, and was tasked with escorting convoys to Europe. After the war she brought troops home and became the flagship of the ships guarding the Navy's seaplanes flying across the Atlantic. In the 1920s she served off the east coast of North, Central and South America. In 1932 the old ship headed for a final tour of duty on the Asiatic Station. Decommissioned at Cavite on 29 April 1933, the ex-USS *New York* was credited with the longest service span of any comparable ship.

She was towed to Subic Bay and spent the next eight years as an auxiliary power plant and machine shop. In 1938 she was removed from the list of United States naval vessels.

On 14 December 1941 the Japanese bombed Olongapo and by 24 December it was obvious that they would take Subic Bay, so the order was given to destroy the station and withdraw. Olongapo and the base were torched and the ex-USS *New York* was towed out into a deep part of the bay and scuttled.

Located between Alava Pier and the northern end of the airport runway, just 15 minutes by banca from the beach, the ex-USS *New York* now lies on her port side in 27m (89ft) of water. Experienced divers can penetrate the wreck easily, swimming through shoals of minute fish sheltering inside. Occasionally lobsters can be spotted. However, the most impressive feature is that the large 20cm (8 in) guns are still in position and intact at 17m (56ft).

Twisted metal – damage caused by explosions during the scuttling – is clearly evident. Small soft corals, sponges and hydroids are common, and there are quite a lot of lionfish, triggerfish, Spotted Sweetlips, Blue-spotted Ribbontail Rays, fusiliers, batfish and the occasional grouper and barracuda. Diving conditions are generally calm with little current.

THE BUSUANGA AND CORON WRECKS

A miniature version of Truk Lagoon, the area around Busuanga and Coron Islands is littered with World War II Japanese shipwrecks that were sunk by American carrier-based aircraft in preparation for the American landing on Leyte. They are mostly auxiliary fleet rather than warships. Many have now been found in recreational diving depths. Strong currents are rare.

When American Admiral 'Bull' Halsey sent reconnaissance aircraft to photograph the Linapacan Strait and the Calamian islands, an observant mapping officer noticed that some of the islands were moving about – a camouflaged Japanese fleet had

been discovered. As a result, at 09:00 hours on 24 September 1944, Task Force 45 Carrier-based aircraft attacked and sank 24 vessels around Busuanga and Coron Islands.

NANSHIN MARU ❷
Just off the beach on the east side of Malajon Island, the wreck of the *Nanshin Maru* sits upright, but down the sandy slope from the shore. The bow bottoms out at 32m (105ft) and the stern at 20m (66ft). The 45m (148ft) coastal vessel is teeming with small bait-fish, lionfish and larger reef fish.

OKIKAWA MARU ❹
On the outer edge of the Lusteveco Company's Pearl Farm, south of Concepción village on Busuanga Island, the oil tanker *Okikawa Maru* is lying almost level with a slight list to port. This is a good wreck for penetration with the main deck at 16m (52ft) and

Above: A black coral provides shelter for small fish on the wreck of the Japanese provision ship *Irako*, Coron.

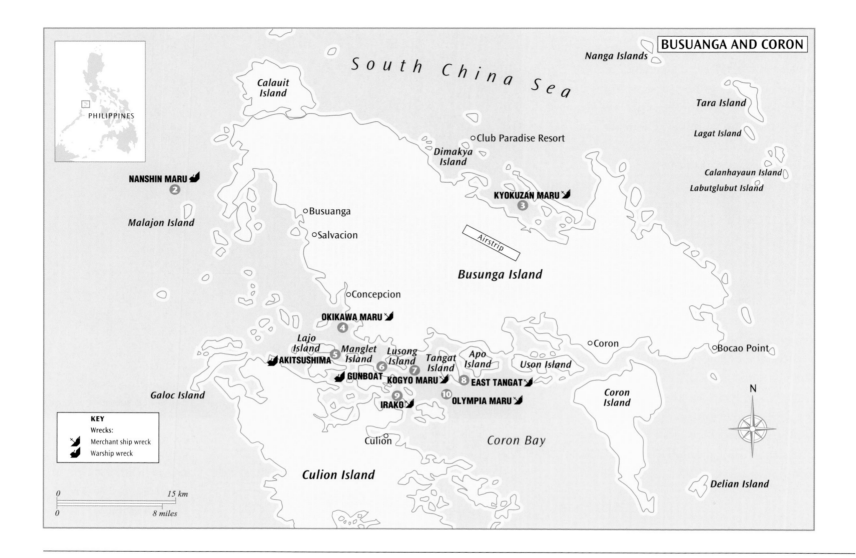

KEY
Wrecks:
Merchant ship wreck
Warship wreck

BUSUANGA AND CORON

South China Sea

Calauit Island

Nanga Islands

Tara Island

Lagat Island

Club Paradise Resort

Calanhayaun Island
Labutglubut Island

Dimakya Island

NANSHIN MARU ❷

KYOKUZAN MARU ❸

Malajon Island

○Busuanga

○Salvacion

Airstrip

Busunga Island

○Concepcion

OKIKAWA MARU ❹

○Coron

○Bocao Point

Lajo Island

Manglet Island

Lusong Island

Tangat Island

Apo Island

Uson Island

AKITSUSHIMA ❺

GUNBOAT ❻

KOGYO MARU ❼

❽ EAST TANGAT

Coron Island

Galoc Island

❾ IRAKO

❿ OLYMPIA MARU

N

Culion

Coron Bay

Culion Island

Delian Island

0   15 km
0   8 miles

a maximum depth of 26m (85ft). This ship was damaged in the first raid, and sunk in a second raid on 9 October. The fact that it was sunk by bombing is very obvious. There are good corals, sponges and fish, including the ubiquitous lionfish and scorpionfish.

AKITSUSHIMA ❺
One of the few true warships found so far, the *Akitsushima* is between Lajo Island and Manglet Island. A 148m (486ft) flying boat tender, she lies on her port side in 38m (125ft) of water with the

starboard side at 20m (66ft). Her recovery crane is broken off. The vessel is broken apart near the stern, so the ship can be penetrated with care. However, this is an advanced dive due to the depth. Large groupers and fry lurk in the hull, and shoals of barracuda, tuna and snapper are found along it.

GUNBOAT ❻
At the southern end of Lusong Island there is the shallow wreck of a gunboat that has been salvaged. The stern breaks the surface at low tide and the maximum depth is 10m (33ft).

KOGYO MARU ❼

East of the southeast corner of Lusong Island, the 158m (518ft) Japanese Freighter *Kogyo Maru* lies on her starboard side at 34m (112ft), with the port side at 22m (72ft).

IRAKO ❾

South of the *Kogyo Maru*, the 147m (482ft) Japanese refrigerated provision ship, *Irako*, is almost upright in 42m (138ft) of water, with the main deck at 28–34m (92–112ft). Because of the depth, penetration is an advanced dive, but the superstructure has soft corals, sponges and profuse fish life. Penetrating to the galley is an impressive, but tricky, dive.

OLYMPIA MARU ❿

West of the southwest end of Tangat Island, the wreck thought to be the 137m (449ft) Japanese Freighter *Olympia Maru* is lying on her starboard side at 25m (82ft) with her port side at 12m (39ft). This site is a good introduction to wreck diving for novices and has good marine life.

EAST TANGAT WRECK ❽

No one is sure of the true name of the 40m (131ft), East Tangat wreck. She lies at the southeast side of Tangat Island, partly salvaged and listing to starboard down a sandy slope. The stern is at 22m (72ft) and the top of the bow at 3m (10ft).

KYOKUZAN MARU ❸

North of Busuanga Island, the 152m (499ft) Japanese Freighter *Kyokuzan Maru* is also known as the Dimilanta Wreck because she is close to the shore at Dimilanta Island. She lies almost upright in 43m (141ft) of water with a milky-white, mist-like haze being released by the cargo in some holds. Almost intact and easily penetrated, the main deck slopes from 22 to 28m (72 to 92ft).

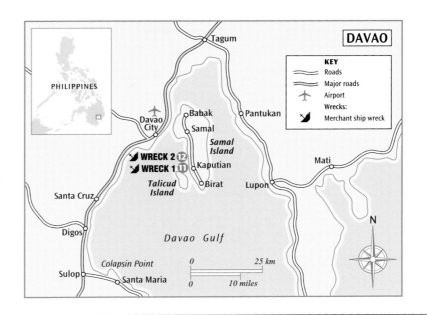

DAVAO – PEARL FARM BEACH RESORT

Pearl Farm Beach Resort has two very good wrecks just in front of the accommodation bungalows, which can only be dived if you are staying at the resort.

Marked by the furthest marker/mooring buoy from the Pearl Farm jetty there is a World War II Japanese freighter (11). The 40m (131ft) vessel is lying on the sand at 35m (115ft), with her mast from 20–27m (66–89ft). The wreck is covered in marine organisms, sponges, shoals of small fry, jacks, lionfish, scorpionfish, batfish, pufferfish, Copperband Butterflyfish and moray eels. An easy ship for penetration by trained divers, it is also good for photography.

Next to the above wreck and marked by the nearest marker/mooring buoy to the Pearl Farm jetty there is a slightly smaller World War II Japanese freighter (12). The 35m (115ft) vessel is lying on her side on the sand at 28 (92ft). Not quite as good a dive as the larger wreck here, she is also covered in marine organisms, feather stars, sponges, shoals of small fry, jacks, lionfish, scorpionfish, Copperband Butterflyfish and moray eels.

CHUUK

By Jack Jackson

WRECKS FEATURED

- ★HEIAN MARU
- ★FUJIKAWA MARU
- ★SHINKOKU MARU
- ★SANKISAN MARU
- ★FUMITZUKI
- ★YAMAGIRI MARU
- ★NIPPO MARU
- ★AIKOKU MARU
- ★SAN FRANCISCO MARU

The State of Chuuk, which was known as Truk or Hogoleu until 1986, comprises seven major island groups lying within the Eastern Caroline Islands southeast of Guam. Part of the Federated States of Micronesia, the islands are enclosed within an encircling barrier of some 69 sand and coral islets, giving a sheltered lagoon 65km (40 miles) in diameter and 2,129km^2 (822 square miles) in area. It was an ideal anchorage, logistic and strategic staging naval and air base for the Japanese fleet in the Central Pacific during World War II. On 17–18 February 1944, a US carrier-based aerial assault, codenamed Operation Hailstorm, from Task Force 58, sank some 60 vessels and downed hundreds of aircraft.

Opposite: The wreck of the *Nippo Maru* is generally in good condition with plenty of artefacts.

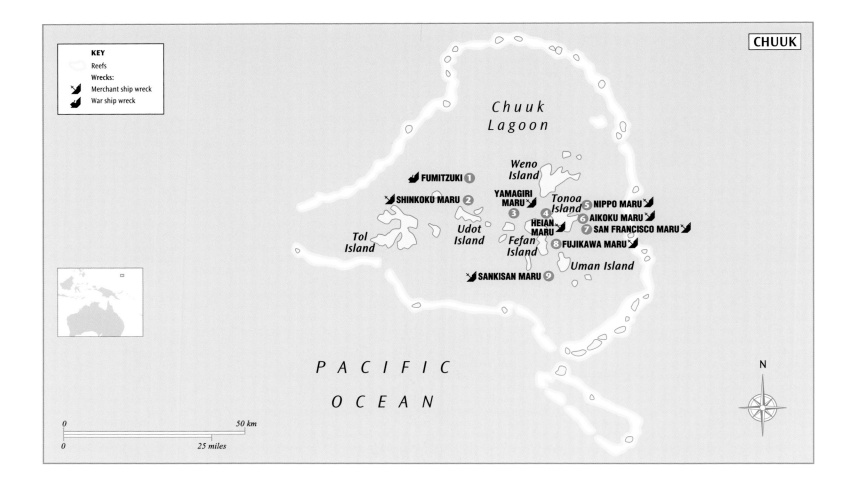

KEY

Reefs

Wrecks:

Merchant ship wreck

War ship wreck

CHUUK

Chuuk Lagoon

FUMITZUKI ❶

SHINKOKU MARU ❷

Weno Island

YAMAGIRI MARU ❸

Tonoa Island

NIPPO MARU ❺

AIKOKU MARU ❻

HEIAN MARU ❹

SAN FRANCISCO MARU ❼

Tol Island

Udot Island

Fefan Island

FUJIKAWA MARU ❽

Uman Island

SANKISAN MARU ❾

PACIFIC OCEAN

0   50 km

0   25 miles

N

The sight of reconnaissance aircraft in advance of the raid had alerted the Japanese and true warships escaped to Palau. This left only the merchant fleet, carrying badly needed supplies for the garrison on Chuuk, together with ships that were under repair.

After a follow-up attack on 29 April 1944, the Truk 'fortress' was reduced to rubble on land as well as at sea, and the 'Ghost Fleet of Truk Lagoon' has since become a magnet for wreck divers. The combination of warm water and tidal currents has transformed these once proud warships with broken hulls and twisted scraps of metal into wonderful artificial reefs adorned with soft and stony corals. Some of the wrecks are too deep for conventional

diving on air, but most are accessible to divers of all standards. Bear in mind that all these wrecks contain human remains, which should be treated with respect.

In the ship names below, *Maru* is used for commercial freighters and passenger vessels. Maru refers to a round trip, which commercial vessels are expected to complete.

HEIAN MARU ❹

The 11,614 ton *Heian Maru* was built by the Osaka Iron Works. The 157m (514ft) passenger/freighter had a beam of 20m (66ft) and is the largest known intact ship in the Lagoon. Requisitioned in World War II, she carried cargo and was used as a submarine tender. Today the *Heian Maru* is lying on her port side in 34–40m (112–131ft) of water and still has a large amount of ordnance, including large torpedoes and shells. Divers can penetrate the engine room and galley. The damaged bridge area is very open and the holds contain periscopes and piles of crockery. The starboard hull is reached at 12m (39ft), and previous divers have collected several artefacts and laid them on the side for photographs. The well-cleaned ship's name is set out in large raised letters, in both English and Japanese script.

FUJIKAWA MARU ❽

One of the signature wrecks of the lagoon, the 6,938 ton *Fujikawa Maru* was built in Tokyo by Mitsubishi in 1938 and requisitioned by the Japanese Navy two years later. The 132m (433ft) armed passenger/freighter had a beam of 18m (58ft). She now sits upright on the bottom of the seabed. The bridge is at 15m (49ft), the deck at 18m (59ft) and the keel at 35m (115ft). The vessel took several hits from bombs and torpedoes, and fire gutted her interior before she sank. The *Fujikawa Maru* is one of the most beautiful wrecks in the lagoon and it needs several dives to see everything. There is lush coral growth on the bow, the derricks and the mast. The wreck carries various types of ordnance; stripped fighter aircraft bodies; aircraft engines and spare parts; Dai Nippon Beer bottles; ceramic electrical parts; shoes; uniforms; and gas masks. Divers can penetrate to the baths, staterooms, galley, engine room and machine shop.

In 1974 a Japanese delegation placed a small shrine on top of the bridge with the names of the crew members.

SHINKOKU MARU ❷

Another of the best wrecks in the lagoon is the 10,020 ton *Shinkoku Maru*. The 165m (541ft) commercial oil tanker had a beam of 20m (65ft) and was built in Kobe in 1940. She was sunk by a

torpedo and now sits upright in 40m (131ft) of water, draped in an amazing variety of soft corals and harbouring large shoals of glassfish. There are large guns fore and aft. The gun at the bow and the top of the bridge are at 12m (39ft) and there are lots of personal belongings. Divers can reach an operations room, where there are typewriters, telephones, and 78rpm vinyl records. Because of her size the *Shinkoku Maru* requires several dives to cover her properly and this is a good wreck for a night dive. The masts used to protrude above the surface, but were demolished to prevent ships from snagging them. Despite being visible from the surface, the wreck's location was forgotten until it was 'rediscovered' in 1971.

Above: The main mast of the *Fujikawa Mara* against the sun.

SANKISAN MARU ❾

Another beautiful dive, the 4,752 ton *Sankisan Maru* was built in America in 1920. The 111m (364ft) freighter had a 16m (53ft) beam. She changed owners and names several times until 1942 when, as the *Estero*, she was captured by the Japanese. She was attacked several times in Chuuk (Truk) Lagoon until she was finally torpedoed in the aft section, setting off the stored ordnance and blowing the aft section away from bridge to stern. In 1974 depth charges and a large bomb were removed to make the wreck safer for divers.

The shattered remains of the stern are now in 50m (164ft) of water, but the forward section is almost intact and upright, and covered in various coloured soft corals. The foremast, covered with soft and stony corals and sponges, reaches to within 5m (16ft) of the surface and the upper deck is at roughly 18m (59ft). The holds have aircraft engines, ammunition, medicine bottles and spare parts.

FUMITZUKI ❶

A true warship, if very old, the 1,772 ton *Fumitzuki* was built in 1925. The Mutsuki Class Destroyer was 103m (339ft) long, with a beam of 9m (30ft), and was capable of 37 knots.

The *Fumitzuki* was shot up badly, limped to Truk Lagoon in the weeks before the raid, and was anchored in the repair anchorage as Operation Hailstorm started. The crew managed to get her under way on only one engine, but that was destroyed by a bomb that flooded the engine compartment, so she was abandoned. She sank in 38m (125ft) of water and settled with a 20–25 degree list to port.

The guns and torpedo launchers are still in place and the guns and davits have lots of soft and stony corals. Gas masks, ceramic ware and bullets can be found, as can rail tracks for the torpedo-loading trolley. This wreck was discovered through the efforts of Tomoyuki Yoshimura, who interviewed survivors

and the ship's captain. He finally located the wreck in April 1987.

YAMAGIRI MARU ❸

The 6,438 ton *Yamagiri Maru* was built by Mitsubishi. The 133m (437ft) freighter had a beam of 17.7m (58ft) and was run by Yamashita Kisen Lines until requisitioned for war service. She then became an ammunition ship for the battleship Musahi. The large shells, measuring 36cm (14 inches), can still be found in this wreck. Almost intact, she now lies on her port side in 34m (112ft) of water. The starboard side is at 15m (49ft) and the ship is draped with colourful soft corals, while shady areas have shoals of glassfish. The wreck is fairly easy to penetrate. Other artefacts include motorcycle parts, tyres, loading equipment, machinery, air compressors, steam rollers, cement mixers and large drums.

NIPPO MARU ❺

The 3,764 ton *Nippo Maru* was built by Kawasaki Dockyards in 1936 as an oil tanker for the Okazaki Kisen Line. She was 106m (348ft) long and had a 15m (50ft) beam. The china found on the wreck still has the Okazaki Kisen insignia. The Japanese Navy requisitioned her in late 1941 and used her to transport water, ordnance and other supplies to the outlying islands of Truk Lagoon, where freshwater was scarce. First found by Jacques-Yves Cousteau's team in 1969, she was then 'lost' until rediscovered on 16 June 1980 by Klaus Lindemann.

Another great dive, today she sits on the bottom in good condition, with a slight list to port. The bow is at 24m (79ft) and the stern at 44m (144ft). There is a torpedo hole in the port engine room. There are lots of artefacts, including large guns that were both the ship's armament and cargo; other ordnance; water tanks; gas masks; bottles; barrels; electric motors and wiring; a battle tank; trucks; spare anchors; medicine boxes; radio equipment; and personal effects. The battle tank, minus its turret gun (which is how they were sometimes transported) is at 35m (115ft), and the bridge is photogenic.

AIKOKU MARU ❻

The 10,437 ton, 152m (498ft) *Aikoku Maru* was built in 1939 to transport passengers and goods for the Osaka Company. She was soon requisitioned by the Japanese Imperial Navy, armed and used for patrol and troopship activities because of her speed.

At the time of her sinking she was carrying a quantity of high explosives in the forward holds and a large number of troops of the 1st Amphibious Brigade, destined for the Marshall Islands. A bomb hit the explosives and most of the troops died from the resulting explosion, which blew off the entire forward section.

Lying almost upright in 64m (210ft) of water, this is one of the deepest dives in the lagoon. The bridge is at 40m (131ft) and the deck at 50m (164ft). A large, photogenic anti-aircraft gun is located on top of the aft deckhouse, and the ship is covered in a profusion of corals and sponges. Penetration is possible, but remember the depth. Under the promenade deck, the galley is full of kitchen utensils.

This wreck was first dived by members of Jacques-Yves Cousteau's team in 1969, but at that time the wreck was not identified. The remains of most of the troops and crew were recovered by a Japanese delegation in 1984. They were partly buried and partly cremated according to the Shinto religion, and a plaque to their memory was placed on the deck.

SAN FRANCISCO MARU ❼

One of the most photographed wrecks in the lagoon, because of three tanks on the deck against the bridge, the 5,831 ton *San Francisco Maru* was built in 1919 by Kawasaki Shipyards in Kobe. The 117m (384ft) freighter was built for Y.K. Lines (probably Nippon Yusen Kaisha). Requisitioned for the Japanese Imperial Navy, she was attacked repeatedly, caught

fire and sank on an even keel in 65m (213ft) of water. The locals refer to her as the Million Dollar Wreck, both for the assortment of her cargo of war supplies and their probable monetary value.

Located in 1973, she requires several dives to do her justice. At roughly 45m (158ft) to the deck, 52m (171ft) to the stern and 58m (190ft) to the bottom of the forward hold, she is fairly intact. There is not as much coral growth, as is the case on other wrecks in the lagoon, but the ship is out of salvage range for most of the locals.

The *San Francisco Maru* has one battle tank on deck forward of the bridge on the port side, and two more on the starboard side. In the holds there are trucks, cars, mines, depth charges, bombs, torpedoes and aircraft parts.

Above: A hand-wheel control in the engine room of the *Yamagiri Maru*.

VANUATU

By Jack Jackson

WRECK FEATURED

★SS PRESIDENT
COOLIDGE

Consisting of four main islands among 83 islands, the archipelago of

Vanuatu, formally known as the New Hebrides, is a blend of tribal

communities, resorts, beaches, volcanoes and pristine underwater

environments. During the course of World War II, over 100,000

allied troops and support staff were stationed here as part of the

American assault to regain islands from the Japanese, including

Guadalcanal. The rotting remains of their war materials can still be

found in the thick jungle, and below the sea at Million Dollar Point

divers can view the legacy of thousands of tonnes of war surplus

dumped by the American forces before leaving. Once part of an

operation to supply these forces, the main attraction to divers is the

President Coolidge off Espiritu Santo, Vanuatu's largest island.

Opposite: A diver gives
scale to one of the guns
on the wreck of the SS
President Coolidge.

SS PRESIDENT COOLIDGE ❶

The largest easily accessible shipwreck in the world, the SS *President Coolidge* was one of two luxury passenger liners constructed for the Dollar Steamship Line in 1929. They were part-subsidized by the US Government because they were intended to carry mail. The SS *President Hoover* was launched on 6 December 1930 by Mrs Herbert Hoover. The SS *President Coolidge* was launched on 21 February 1931 by President Coolidge's widow, Mrs Grace Coolidge. As this was during Prohibition, when champagne was not available, Mrs Coolidge smashed a bottle of water from her husband's Vermont farm against the hull.

The 199m (654ft) *President Coolidge* was built by Newport News Shipbuilding Drydock Company in Newport News, Virginia, USA. She had a 25m (81ft) beam and displaced 21,936 tons. She was powered by a Westinghouse Electric and Manufacturing Company turbine-electric propulsion system: 12 Babcock and Wilcox high pressure boilers, heated by fuel oil, sent steam to two 14,000 brake horsepower turbines, and each then turned a 10,200 kilowatt generator. The 4,000 volts of three-phase electricity from these generators was then sent to two 13,250 horsepower electric motors that each drove a propeller.

When the *President Coolidge* was delivered to the Dollar Line on 1 October 1931, she and the *President Hoover* were the largest passenger ships constructed in America at that time. The *President Coolidge* operated as a luxury liner carrying 990 passengers and 324 crew, mostly on trans-Pacific routes where she broke several speed records on trips to Japan from San Francisco. The ship was decorated in Art Deco style and no expense was spared on the lavish furnishings in the public rooms, staterooms and lounges. She even had two swimming pools – the first-class one was permanent and the other was a removable canvas structure that fitted as a hatch cover on a hold. She also had seven cargo holds, one

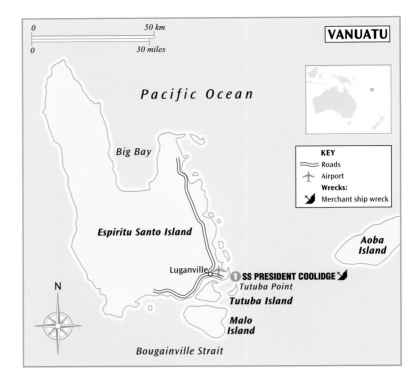

of which was refrigerated, and cars could be loaded through side-ports.

Although the Dollar Line survived the Great Depression, it was not all smooth sailing. On 6 March 1937, while outbound from San Francisco, the *President Coolidge* struck and sank the oil tanker *Frank H. Buck* near the Golden Gate Bridge. On 11 December 1937, the *President Hoover* ran aground near Hoishoto Island off the southern tip of Taiwan and was declared a total loss. On 3 June 1938 the *President Coolidge* was arrested in San Francisco for an unpaid debt of $35,000. A bond was raised but the Dollar Line's days were numbered and ownership of the President Coolidge passed on to the US Government. On 1 November 1938, the name of the company was changed to American President Lines Ltd.

For the next three years the *Coolidge* continued to sail the Pacific and in mid-1940 was used to evacuate Americans from China and Japan. She assisted in evacuating many people from Asia as the Japanese increased their aggression. On 7 December 1941 the Japanese attacked Pearl Harbor and America entered World War II. The *President Coolidge*, chartered and operated by the War Shipping Administration for the US Army, was stripped of her finery, painted grey, mounted with guns and converted into a troopship that could carry over 5,000 personnel.

In 1942 the *President Coolidge* was heading for Luganville, in present-day Vanuatu when, on the morning of 26 October, just a short distance from her destination, she struck a 'friendly' American mine. Soon after, she struck a second one in the east entrance of the Segond Channel at Espiritu Santo. The captain tried to save the vessel by driving onto the reef, but she continued to take on water and, in 90 minutes, slipped off and sank. Of the 5,440 troops and crew on board, only four died.

After the war, salvage operations recovered items such as the propeller blades, the brass casings of shells, 600 tons of oil from bunkers and copper tubing. However, on 18 November 1983 the Vanuatu government declared that no further salvage or recovery of any artefact would be allowed from the *Coolidge*.

The ship now lies on her port side a short distance from shore near the town of Luganville. The bow is the shallowest point at 15m (49ft) and the stern is the deepest at 70m (230ft). Being so large and in parts so deep, divers require as many as ten dives to cover her properly. Those new to the wreck can start without any penetration by swimming underneath and around the bow and along the starboard side, looking at the prolific marine life and her sheer size. For easy penetration swim along the promenade deck and see the ship's massive 76mm (3 inch) gun, ordnance, gas masks and troops' toilets, with their total lack of privacy.

A favourite with many divers is 'The Lady and the Unicorn'. Discovered in 1981, this ceramic figure of a woman with a unicorn used to stand above a marble fireplace, down one level at 45m (148ft), at the far

end of the First Class Smoking Room. A large part of it broke away during an earth tremor, but local dive operators gathered the broken pieces together, rebuilt the ceramic and repositioned it in a more accessible place for visiting divers. They bolted it to the ceiling of the First Class Dining Saloon at 39m (128ft). For moderate penetration, the captain's bathroom, with some personal belongings, has a maximum depth of 39m (128ft). On the bottom, at around 42m (138ft), there are 20mm (¾ inch) guns and the massive anchor lies in the sand. From the mosaic-tiled first-class swimming pool, divers can swim though the main lounge area and exit through the bridge.

The holds contain all sorts of military equipment, including a General Motors Corporation truck, Jeeps and tracked vehicles. The engine room is entered through a large hole cut by the salvors. For those with enough training to dive the depth at the stern, one can descend down a shot-line to the propeller shafts and rudder.

Most dives on the *President Coolidge* are treated as decompression dives, with spare SCUBA cylinders of air or Nitrox hung at 5 and 9m (16 and 30ft) or deeper, on a shot-line down to the bow. Local dive masters have fed the fish here, so they now approach divers expectantly.

Below: The ceramic 'The Lady and the Unicorn' was broken during an earth tremor, but it has now been repaired and moved to a shallower location for divers, SS *President Coolidge*.

SOLOMON ISLANDS

By Andy Belcher

Struggling through a period of civil unrest has meant that for a few years the Solomon Islands have been low on divers' lists of destinations. However, their wrecks are among the best dives. Unrest is not unfamiliar to these islands. During World War II the Solomon Islands became a turning point in the bitter struggle by the allied forces to repel the Japanese in the Pacific. By March 1942 the Japanese had already advanced as far south as Rabaul and Bougainville and were advancing to the Solomons, where they eventually landed at Gavutu and Tulagi, and finally on Guadalcanal, the main island in the group. Their intention was to build an airbase from which to attack other groups of islands and cut the lines of communication to Australia. The Americans, despite their efforts, suffered a disastrous defeat at sea, and the stretch of water between the island of Savo and Guadalcanal, littered with about 40 wrecks, is now known as Iron Bottom Sound.

Opposite: Two 12.7mm (1/2 inch) calibre bullets sent this American Grumman Hellcat to a watery grave. It now lies, virtually intact, in only 12m (39ft) of water, west of Gizo.

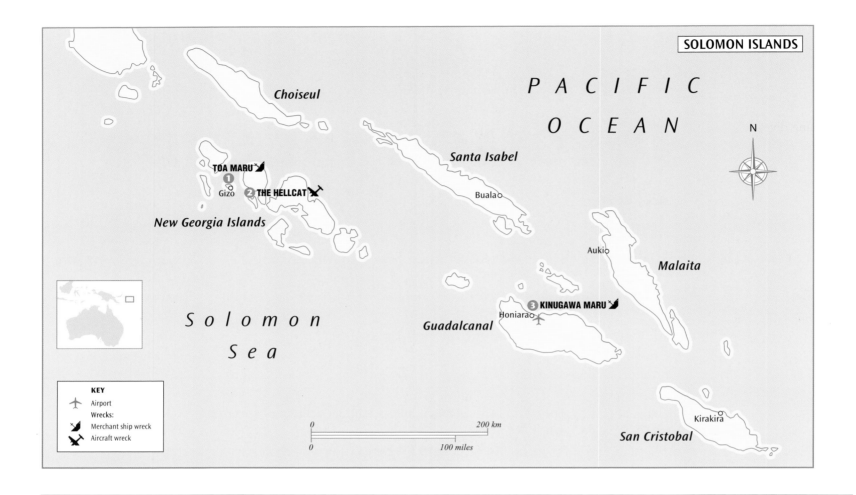

SOLOMON ISLANDS

P A C I F I C

O C E A N

N

Choiseul

Santa Isabel

Bualao

TOA MARU
❶
Gizo
❷ **THE HELLCAT**

New Georgia Islands

Aukio

Malaita

S o l o m o n

S e a

❸ **KINUGAWA MARU**
Honiarao

Guadalcanal

Kirakira

San Cristobal

KEY
✈ Airport
Wrecks:
🛦 Merchant ship wreck
🛦 Aircraft wreck

0   200 km
0   100 miles

US forces eventually took control of the airport and gained air supremacy. Further attempts were made by the Japanese to land troops and supplies, but the American aircraft assumed control of all ship movements by day and regular bombing runs left many of the freighters on fire and running themselves onto the beach to unload supplies. Just one of the legacies left from the war is the abundance of ship and aircraft dives within safe diving depths around the Solomon Islands.

KINUGAWA MARU ❸

Twenty minutes' drive or just a short boat ride from the country's capital of Honiara, the unsightly view of rusting superstructure breaking the surface of the water gives away the location of the *Kinugawa Maru*. The wreck is also known as Bonegi Two after the nearby Bonegi River.

What can be seen beneath the surface is anything but unsightly. A floral wreath as far as the eye can see, this wreck epitomizes the phrase 'there is life after death'. Soft corals begin in as little as 3m (10ft) and are surrounded by scores of small colourful fish, the coral growth and fish numbers increasing prolifically as you descend.

The 132m (433ft) *Kinugawa Maru*'s stern rests in 24m (79ft) of water, the crumpled bow rammed into the steeply shelving beach making it an ideal wreck for both snorkelling and scuba-diving. Beneath the surface, strong tropical sunlight beams through frames and girders of the ships' mid-sections, creating a gothic cathedral effect, while cascades of fish weave through the iron struts. Tall ladders stretch skywards and huge cooking woks, encrusted with coral, lie idle on the decks. Photographically it is a stunning dive. At 24m (79ft), where the rudder and propshaft rest on the sand alongside giant black corals and large basket sponges, a glance along the side of the ship towards the surface will leave you with an unforgettable image.

The dive is suitable for beginner to intermediate. There is sometimes current and it can have swell or surface chop.

TOA MARU ❶

One of the larger, more intact and easily accessible monuments of war, the 6,866 tonne Japanese freighter *Toa Maru* lies off the north coast of Gizo Island. She can be acccessed by boat.

On 31 January 1943 an American air strike was ordered against the Japanese shipping in Vella Gulf. The 137m (450ft) *Toa Maru* was strafed by a Wildcat squadron, and the cargo of fuel and oil carried in the rear cargo hold caught fire. The vessel became a burning inferno, and the order was given to abandon ship. Local rumour says that the ship drifted for approximately three days before running aground on Kololuka Island, where she finally filled with water and sank. She rolled onto her starboard side, with her bow at 12m (39ft) and stern at 40m (131ft).

When the visibility is good the *Toa Maru* can be seen from the surface, her huge bulk casting what seems like a giant shadow on the ocean floor. Outside the wreck on the seafloor it is hard not to miss the skeletons of trucks, tanks, ammunition and a plethora of assorted remains, which have become a garden for corals and marine life.

Penetration dives will take you down past the galley with its huge ovens, steam woks and noodle makers. The vast engine room is littered with fire extinguishers, oil cans, broken cabling, huge valves and wiring panels. The crockery room still has stacks of plates and cups. The various cargo holds contain an upturned tank, motorbike, mortars, rifles and munitions. The rear half shows signs of immense heat: buckled girders, charred timbers, metal and glass. The diving is exciting and warrants more than one visit. For wreck enthusiasts there is much still to be uncovered. The depth of the dive is 12–27m (39–89ft) and currents are rare. Intermediate diving skills are required.

THE HELLCAT ❷

Further to the west of Gizo, on the edge of Blackett Strait, lies an American Grumman Hellcat (F6F-3 fighter plane). It is virtually intact and makes a relaxing and fascinating dive in only 12m (39ft) of water. The Hellcat was accidentally shot down by a compatriot on 6 October 1943, but the wreckage was not located until 1985.

The plane took two 12.7mm (½ inch) calibre bullets, one in the port side of the engine and the other aft of the cockpit. After the engine quit, the pilot, Dick Moore, stalled the aircraft full flaps down and landed in the water without difficulty. Not long after Moore had inflated his lifejacket, two large canoes containing 21 natives and a US private, rescued him. Everything that was in the plane on the day it was ditched still remains. You can easily slip into the cockpit and let your imagination take over, eyes darting around the liquid blue while silver mackerels dart around like enemy fighters. It is great fun and good visibility means that the 14m (46ft) long plane can be seen from the surface and quite easily snorkelled. In fact, it is so easily snorkelled that the last time I dived the Hellcat, I was surprised to see very little coral growth on the wreck and its metal exterior was nearly gleaming. Apparently the local natives had snorkelled down to scrub it so it would look good for visiting divers!

The wreck can be accessed by boat and is suitable for novices. There is rarely any current.

PAPUA NEW GUINEA

By Bob Halstead

Famous for its lush reefs and unbeatable biodiversity, Papua New Guinea can add great wreck diving to its attractions. Over a dozen modern wrecks of coastal traders or fishing boats have been deliberately sunk to make artificial reefs for divers. The largest divable wreck, the *Maritime Hibiscus* at 11,000 tonnes, was a logging ship that accidentally struck a reef before sinking. However, the most popular wreck dives are relics from World War II. There are a few wonderful shipwrecks, a couple of mini-submarines and many aircraft wrecks. Some of these aircraft were carefully ditched and remain in near perfect condition on the seabed. The best of these is the B17 Bomber Blackjack, a huge intact aircraft that had an incredible war history. What no one realized until September of 2004 was that just an hour away was a marvellous P38 Lightning wreck with no war history at all.

Opposite: The B17 Bomber Blackjack lies in 46m (151ft) of usually clear water. Its nose, which still has a machine gun, was damaged when it glided into the sandy seabed.

LOCKHEED P-38 F LIGHTNING FIGHTER, 42-12649 ❶

This aircraft was safely ditched by its pilot, Captain Porter, eight months before Blackjack's (see below) ditching. The Lockheed P-38 Lightning was a twin-engined, single-seater fighter with distinctive twin-boom fuselages containing each engine. The armament consisted of four 12.7mm (½-inch) calibre machine guns and one 20mm (¾inch) cannon, all housed in the nose section ahead of the pilot's cockpit. These are visible in the wreck, as are all the cockpit gauges and controls and the heavy armour plate that protected the pilot's back. Landing gear, with tyre still in place, can be seen beneath the starboard fuselage, now covered in multicoloured sponges. The P38 was a leap forward in aircraft design. Both engines were turbocharged and they could out-run the feared Japanese Zero fighter that dominated at the start of World War II.

Comparing the war records of the two aircraft, they could hardly have been more different – Blackjack fought and survived many missions, but the P-38 was ditched on a delivery voyage and had not fired a shot in anger. In contrast to Blackjack, the P-38 is in only 12–17m (39–56ft) of calm, still water. It is, however, also perfectly intact and, in addition, is festooned with corals and colourful sponges.

BLACKJACK ❷

The Boeing B17 Flying Fortress bomber was affectionately nicknamed Blackjack after the '21' at the end of its call sign, 41-24521. Blackjack was considered a charmed aircraft with a colourful history in the Pacific campaign, but its charm failed on 11 July 1943. Taking off from Port Moresby just after midnight, with a crew of ten and a full load of bombs, Blackjack set course for its target at Rabaul. With the heavy load the aircraft struggled to get enough height to clear the mountains of the Owen Stanley Range and had to circle three times. Then, when it was finally able to cross, bad weather caused

the flight gyro to malfunction. The crew, led by pilot Lt Ralph DeLoach, pushed on and eventually found themselves in Kimbe Bay with an easy course to Rabaul. But here their hearts sank as both engines on the starboard side of the aircraft failed. One was vibrating so badly that it threatened to rip the engine from its mount. The weather got even worse, and it became a struggle to keep the aircraft flying. Nevertheless, vulnerable to night fighters and ground fire, the crew completed their bombing run with the crippled plane and only then turned for home.

Fighting to get enough power to skim clear of the mountains of New Britain, Blackjack ran into another violent storm and became completely lost. At 05:00 their altitude was 1,525m (5,000ft) and they were not able to climb out of the storm. At 06:15 fuel was becoming low and they were still in the storm and now at an altitude of only 610m (2,000ft). Everything movable was thrown from the aircraft and the crew was told to prepare for a water landing. At 07:00

Blackjack broke out of the storm and in the early morning light an unknown coastline came into view. Heading southeast towards allied territory, the crew had barely enough fuel to select a beach on which to crash-land. At 07:20, with great difficulty, Blackjack was guided to a shallow reef, only to skip over it and settle into deep water just off a large village.

The pilot and co-pilot exited through the cockpit windows, while the rest of the crew, including one who was badly injured, scrambled out through the main hatch and onto the one life raft that had inflated. Within 45 seconds of hitting the water, Blackjack had sunk. With the injured man in the raft and the others hanging on the side, the raft started to drift out to sea. However, after all of the bad luck, some good luck was due: it turned out that Blackjack had not only reached allied territory, but one of the friendliest villages on the whole coast. Boga Boga villagers jumped into their canoes and rushed to help. Soon all were ashore and safe.

Underwater, Blackjack nose-dived down a steep coral cliff, banged into the sand bottom at 46m (151ft) and settled back, its port tailplane tip bending up on a sloping coral outcrop at the base of the cliff. The bottom gun turret was smashed up into the fuse-lage on impact and it was here that crew were injured. Otherwise, the aircraft remained completely intact, the four engines and 31m (102ft) wingspan stretched over the sand just as if it had been parked there.

In 1986 dive adventurer Rod Pearce was near Boga Boga when villagers told him about 'their' aircraft. Pearce dived down the cliff through clear water to be met with one of the most amazing sights of his extensive diving career. Blackjack was still there and apart from some additional coral and sponge growth, lay undisturbed before him. Guns still swivelled and the inside of the cockpit was visible through the open side windows.

To aid visiting divers, Rod fastened a guideline down the cliff wall. Divers should, however, beware: although all the crew survived the crash, in the 20 years that sport divers have been diving Blackjack, two have lost their lives. The two main hazards are the depth, which at 46m (151ft) is just outside some training agencies' standard maximum dive depths on air, and the current that can reach up to one knot. The water is usually very clear, averaging 40m (131ft), and the fantastic condition and large size of the wreck tempt divers to stay longer than they should.

There is usually time for one complete circuit of the aircraft, starting along the starboard wing towards the dinged nose where a machine gun still pokes, surrounded by small silver baitfish. A good look through the cockpit windows shows all the controls in place. Behind the cockpit, a turret with twin machine guns is pacified by soft corals. An open hatch provides a view of the radio operator's station and another machine gun slung inside. Further aft, side hatches, from which machine guns had been jettisoned, allow a view inside the aircraft to see the broken bottom turret. Do not be tempted to enter, since loose cables hang to trap the unwary.

Right at the stern, beneath the enormous tail and rudder, the rear guns still swivel in their mounts. The starboard tail, bent up, points to the safe exit and ascent line. You need at least half your supply of breathing gas at this point to make a long safe ascent up the slope and then the cliff. Moving gently along the cliff, and keeping it to your right shoulder, you can put in some decompression time and end up in a shallow sandy lagoon, usually accompanied by a school of Bumphead Parrotfish.

The wreck was featured in a documentary film, *Blackjack's Last Mission*, which included historical footage and a return to Boga Boga village by pilot Ralph DeLoach. Blackjack was also featured in the April 1988 *National Geographic* story on *Ghosts of the Pacific*. What no one else realized until September 2004 was that just 22.2km (12 nautical miles) to the east of Boga Boga, off Magabura village, lay the lost and forgotten wreck of the Lockheed P-38 F Lightning fighter, 42-12649.

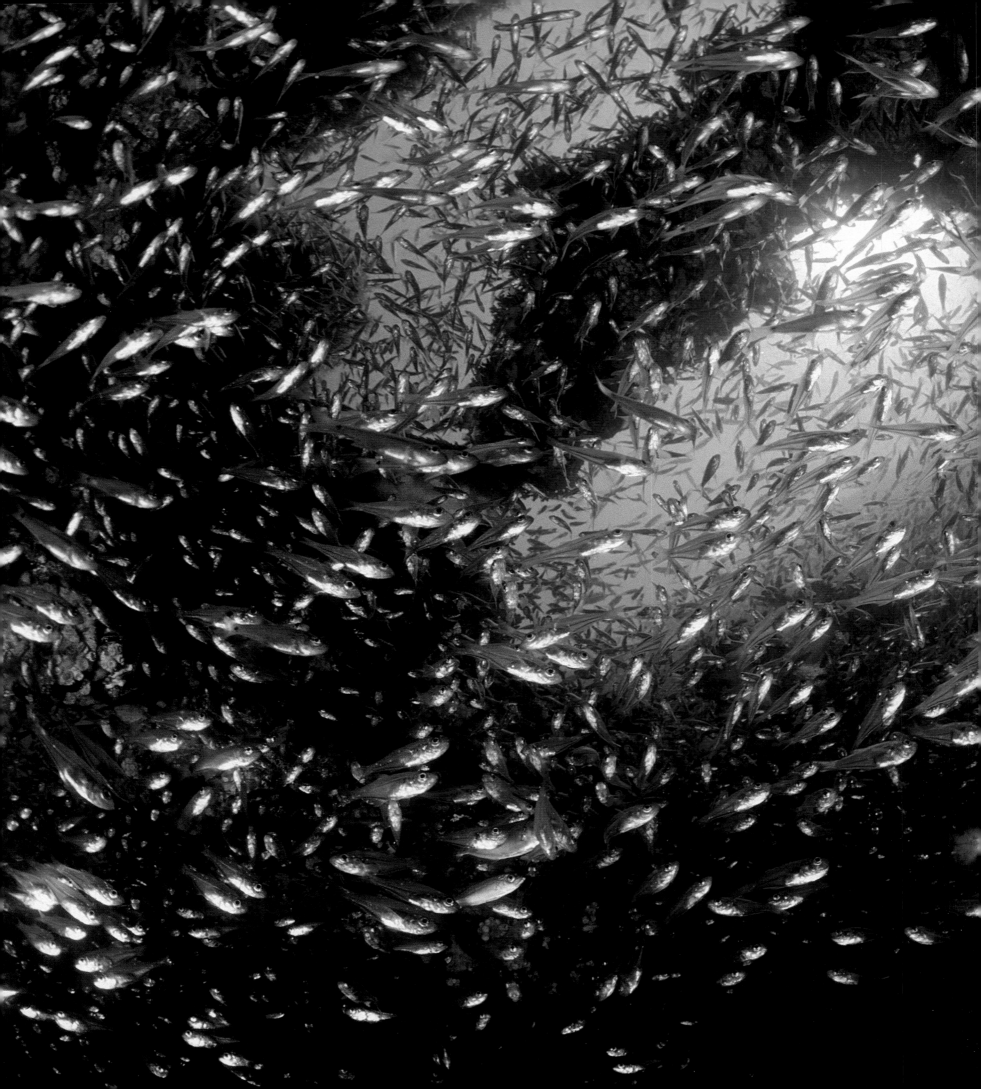

AUSTRALIA – East Coast

By Bob Halstead

A Giant Queensland Grouper on the famous wreck of the *Yongala* had clamped its mouth around the head of a scuba diver, reported the *Townsville Bulletin* of 3 January 2002. The diver claimed 'it went dark' as his head entered the grouper's mouth. There were cuts on his cheeks, neck and shoulders. Other divers told how they were 'targeted by the monster which snuck up behind them despite their attempts to kick it away'. It was front-cover news. Stories were growing faster than the grouper, which had reached at least 2m (6½ft) in length, and would soon reach a size where it could swallow the whole 112m (367ft) *Yongala*. Officious non-diving nincompoops were demanding that the wreck be closed to divers until the threat had been removed.

Opposite: The superstructure of the *Yongala* is full of small fry. These attract many large predators, such as groupers and travallies, which can always be seen on the wreck.

This really took me back to the good old days of Australian diving when giant clams could leap up to grab innocent snorkellers, and sharks were all 4m (12ft) whalers or 8m (25ft) Great Whites that just loved the taste of neoprene. My wife and I immediately booked to dive the *Yongala*.

The SS *Yongala* was owned by the Adelaide Steamship Company, who advertised the vessel as providing 'Magnificent Australian Inter-State Mail Steamship Services'. On 23 March 1911, approaching Townsville on a voyage from Melbourne to Cairns, she was caught in the eye of a cyclone and sank with the loss of a red Lincoln bull, a racehorse named Moonshine and all 121 passengers and crew. The SS *Yongala* was not quite eight years old.

The wreck site is in exposed open water and sometimes it is too rough to dive. There can also be currents and typical inner Great Barrier Reef visibility – i.e. not that great. On the plus side the depths are a reasonable 18–28m (58–92ft) and the wreck attracts fantastic marine life. This marine life is what makes the *Yongala* one of the greatest wreck dives in the world. The wreck is missing its funnel, but is otherwise intact on the flat sandy bottom, with a heavy list to starboard. Dive boats moor up-current of the wreck, usually off its bow, then set a guide line to the hull.

As we moored in the slight current, turtles and sea snakes were making regular excursions to the mirror-calm surface. The water looked surprisingly clear and large schools of fish ghosted below. Bull and Tiger Sharks are said to visit the wreck. It was therefore with interest that, while on the boat, observing the lascivious writhing of a particularly menacing sea snake on the surface, I witnessed a large fish leap from the water and spin several times before plunging back. I thought initially that it was a Spinner Dolphin, but when I saw it the second time I was convinced it was a shark. Referring to my shark manual I discovered that there is a

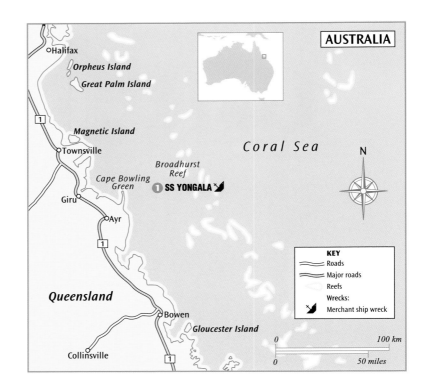

Spinner Shark (*Carcharhinus brevipinna*) that occurs in Australian waters.

It is not unusual to encounter huge jellyfish drifting around the wreck, with their very long, trailing tentacles. Australian sea jellies can cause agonizing pain, and scarring worthy of a horror film. The dive masters warn to watch out for large stingrays that patrol the wreck, and to keep good track of depths and bottom times. Several divers have been bent on the wreck.

Diving on the *Yongala* is an awesome and spectacular experience. Every diver I have spoken to regards it as a quantum leap better than any other wreck dive. On the *Yongala* the fish are often so thick that it is almost impossible to see the wreck at all. They comprise not just the zillions of small fry, but also Giant Trevallies, Mangrove Jacks, batfish, stingrays, Coral Trout, and just about anything you can think of. After I finned my way through the milling throng to get to the wreck, I discovered that

every surface was covered in purple soft coral, black corals, sea whips and marvellous red harp and other exotic corals.

So did we survive? The turtles, feasting on sea jellies caught on the wreck, turned out to be tame; and the sea snakes inspected us, but swam away bored, like burnt-out dive guides. The Bull Shark that I was told later had swum right behind me, was a common Grey Reef Shark; and the sea jelly's sting (I accidentally tried it) was quite mild.

Which brings us to 'Grumpy', as the grouper with an appetite for divers is affectionately called. He is quite a big Giant or Queensland Grouper (*Epinephelus lanceolatus*), but not the biggest on the wreck. Of the four individuals I saw, he was the smallest. I guess he looked more than a metre long. He is, however, a fish with character, and I admire him. Grumpy is interested in divers and not intimidated by them. He did not mouth my camera, as other groupers have done in the past, and did not charge me or nibble on my extremities. He certainly

came very close to me – but I rather enjoyed that. Other divers felt him to be menacing, probably because they were told he was. Although Giant Groupers have been rumoured to attack divers, there has never been a verified fatality. No one can predict that Grumpy will not eventually rough up a diver. Other groupers have, but usually only when they have been fed fish by divers, and no feeding is allowed on the *Yongala*.

The *Yongala* is a protected wreck and not only is no artefact collecting allowed, but neither is any penetration, since the authorities realize that divers' exhaled air inside the wreck will hasten its deterioration. Not so long ago, a visiting diver ignored the warning, ended up in court, and was fined Australian $2,000. I made five dives on my first day, Nitrox ensuring no problems with decompression. It is easy to dive round the whole wreck but, particularly since you cannot penetrate, it is the endless encounters with exciting animals that is the big thrill.

Above: 'Grumpy' is one of several large Queensland Groupers resident on the *Yongala*. He swims close to divers and has been known to be aggressive.

NEW ZEALAND

By Andy Belcher

The coastal regions of New Zealand range from the subtropical north to the cooler climes of the sub-Antarctic in the deep south. Dive sites surrounding the country rival some of the best in the world. There are approximately 160 known and diveable wrecks around New Zealand shores, but it is the more recent wrecks like the large sunken passenger liner *Mikhail Lermontov*, the ex-museum attraction *Taioma* and the sabotaged *Rainbow Warrior* that attract many visiting divers. Other deliberately scuttled wrecks like the HMNZS *Tui* and HMNZS *Waikato* are also drawcards.

Opposite: A classic view of steps on the *Rainbow Warrior* covered in marine growth.

Like most wrecks that have been sunk specifically for recreational diving, both the *Tui* and the *Waikato* are buoyed and rest within reasonable diving depth. Regular dive charters visit the wreck sites. Because of their convenient location close to the Poor Knights Islands (rated among the world's top dive sites), they are a bonus for overseas divers visiting the country.

It is not treasure that entices wreck divers to the sunken remains around New Zealand, although much was found on the *Elingamite* at the Three Kings Islands, and much more eludes divers who still search for the wreck of the *General Grant* at the Auckland Islands. Rather, it is the excitement of underwater photography, the opportunity to collect seafood and New Zealand's commitment to establishing artificial marine reserves as part of its progressive plan to protect and nurture the unique marine flora and fauna surrounding the coast.

Many vessels wrecked on the New Zealand coast have been pounded to pieces by successive storms, with only twisted metal or steel boilers remaining. However, in deeper waters, and at more protected sites, there is still enough wreckage to make the diving interesting.

The stories of three of New Zealand's most popular wrecks are unrelated to the changeable weather that hits the New Zealand coastline.

RAINBOW WARRIOR ❶

The demise of the 40m (131ft) *Rainbow Warrior* is a tale of spies and murder, of clandestine meetings and of international politics. Owned by environmental organization Greenpeace, the *Rainbow Warrior* was docked in Auckland Harbour while activists prepared her for departure to Mururoa Atoll, where they would protest France's plans to continue nuclear testing in the South Pacific.

In the dead of night on 10 July 1985, French secret agents attached two limpet mines to the hull. The mines exploded within minutes of each other,

killing Greenpeace photographer Fernando Pereira and leaving the ship beyond repair. Two of the agents were later arrested, tried and jailed.

As the scandal died down a new controversy emerged. What to do with the *Rainbow Warrior*? After a lifetime campaigning to preserve the environment, it seemed fitting to scuttle her in an area where she would become a living reef. The ship was refloated and after months of lengthy discussions was towed north and was laid to rest southwest of Motutapere Island in the Cavalli Group off Northland.

Within hours of her sinking the first marine creatures had begun to check out this gigantic intruder. Microscopic plants and biological drifters began to settle. Twenty-one years later underwater marine life has woven its threads throughout her bow rails and structure creating a living rainbow of colours.

A permanent mooring buoy marks the spot where the *Rainbow Warrior*'s skeleton lies upright on a

Opposite: A colourful tapestry of anemones coats the *Rainbow Warrior*. The intriguing tale of its demise is one of spies, murder, clandestine meetings and international politics.

sandy ocean floor in 25m (82ft) of water. Silvery curtains of mackerel often drift across her bow while, deeper in the stern, small Red Snappers group. Although the once barren skeleton now harbours many different life forms, there is still a sense of decay. Timber is becoming honeycombed with the borings of shipworms, and metal plates are beginning to corrode and collapse. Divers can still enter the wheelhouse, but it is unsafe to penetrate the wreck. A dive on the *Rainbow Warrior* is a dive onto an important part of New Zealand's historical and political history.

There are organized boat trips from Paihia, Bay of Islands. Depth of the dive is 15–25m (49–82ft), with visibility of about 10m (33ft). There is rarely any current and divers need to be of intermediate level. The nearest hyperbaric chamber is at Auckland Navy Base.

TAIOMA ❷

Built in Scotland in 1942, the 32m (105ft) *Taioma* (formerly the *Empire Jane*) was requisitioned by the Ministry of War Transport for coastal towing service. Following the Normandy landings, the tug performed salvage and rescue operations in the Omaha Beach area before being bought by the Union Steamship Company in New Zealand in 1947. The vessel was renamed *Taioma* and for the next 30 years she worked in Wellington harbour: she was in fact one of the first tugs to try to secure a line to the stricken Inter-Island ferry *Wahine* before that vessel sank with the loss of 51 people's lives on 10 April 1968.

By 1975 the tug had been superseded by more modern vessels and sat idle before being purchased by Tauranga businessman Bob Owen for the princely sum of $2 and towed north to Tauranga. (During a fundraising auction to help pay for the scuttling of the tug, Bob Owen's daughter paid $1,950 for just one of the portholes!) There, the tug was taken ashore as an exhibit at the local historic

museum, where it stood as a memorial to merchant naval men who lost their lives during World War II. When the lease on the museum ran out and the *Taioma* was doomed to become scrap, local divers fought to have the boat taken back out to sea and sunk as an artificial marine reserve. Getting the tug to her watery grave involved the removal of 50 tonnes of weight, closing off and monitoring 5km (3 miles) of motorway and removing two huge overhead pedestrian bridges before she could be towed 22.2km (12 nautical miles) to the designated site, the southeast side of Motiti Island, Bay of Plenty, North Island.

She lies upright on the sand at 28m (92ft), is used for wreck dive training and is an unofficial marine reserve. All hazardous objects and materials have been removed, including the back of the boiler, which enables divers to swim straight down the funnel directly into the boiler room. Areas deemed unsafe were welded shut and a series of holes was cut in the hull to enable natural light to filter through. A steel prop and steering wheel were refitted, replacing the original bronze ones.

The *Taioma* makes the perfect first wreck dive. Descend the shot line near the bow or stern of the boat. The dive time allowed leaves just enough time to explore the ship from end to end, and inside out, before ascending via the shot line. Blue Mao Mao, demoiselles, small snapper and terakihi school above the wreck, while small crustaceans hide within. The hull is covered in bryzoans and small hydroids. This is an interesting dive for both macro and wide-angle photography.

Access is by boat and the depth of the dive is 20–28m (66–92ft). The current is not significant. Divers need to be of intermediate level.

MIKHAIL LERMONTOV ❸

No one knows exactly what possessed the pilot to swing the 20,000 tonne Russian cruise liner *Mikhail Lermontov* into the shallow passage between Cape

Jackson and the Cape Jackson lighthouse at the top of New Zealand's South Island. The pilot's spur-of-the-moment action poses one of the great unanswered questions in the whole of New Zealand's maritime history.

It was a cool, dark, windy night on 17 February 1986 when the 176m (577ft) *Mikhail Lermontov* made her unexpected turn and headed down the 460m (1509ft) wide channel, noisily crunching over rocks and gouging a narrow hole in her starboard side. Managing to clear the channel, she then entered the deeper waters of the mouth of Port Gore. However, water poured into the vessel and gradually it became clear that she was doomed. The 700, mainly elderly, passengers were transferred to local fishing boats, the Cook Strait ferry and an LPG tanker that had rushed to the scene. Miraculously, the only loss of life was a Soviet refrigeration engineer. The $45 million *Mikhail Lermontov* now lies in 30m (98ft) of water and is the largest and most accessible wreck dive in New Zealand.

Descending 10m (33ft) down the permanent shot line to the wreck brings you to its port side, a flat expanse of steel, portholes and windows. The over-riding impression is one of colossal size. Everything is big, except the hole that sank her – a long, narrow split in the hull beginning just astern of the bow thrusters. Exploring the ship's exterior, attractions include the forward anchors; huge propellers astern; radar and navigation gear; the enormous funnel with its classic hammer and sickle; and the deployed lifeboat davits.

Penetration dives need more careful planning. The best areas are those that are open to the sunlight and have obvious entry and exit points. The ballroom, which is always a favourite, spans the entire width of the ship. Because the *Mikhail Lermontov* lies on her side, this huge expanse of flooring now resembles an undersea cliff with tables poking out of it. The swimming pool, which is still enclosed in its glasshouse-type structure, has several entrances and is also interesting. Tables and bars surround the pool and prominent signs read 'No diving please' and 'Caution! The pool is empty'. A ship of this size has many other areas to lure divers. The reality, however, is that anywhere tight and narrow that takes a diver out of sight of his entry point is dangerous. Visibility becomes severely affected by disturbed silt. The depth of the dive is 13–36m (43–118ft), and access is by boat. Only advanced divers should attempt it.

Current is not significant on the wreck, but may be experienced during the ascent and safety stops. Surface conditions can be difficult, with wind and choppy seas.

Below: The largest and most accessible wreck in New Zealand waters, the *Mikhail Lermontov* is imposing.

CANADA – Vancouver Island

By Lawson Wood

The town of Nanaimo, on the east coast of Vancouver Island, has

become one of North America's major centres for wreck diving, due

to the efforts of a group of like-minded British Columbian divers

and conservationists, who banded together as the Artificial Reef

Society of British Columbia (ARSBC) to create a number of artificial

reefs along the British Columbian coast by sinking old or

decommissioned ships, thereby attracting both marine life and dive

tourists to these locations.

Opposite: Part of the
superstructure on the
HMCS *Saskatchewan*.

HMCS SASKATCHEWAN ❶

The centrepiece of the ARSBC's efforts off Nanaimo has been the sinking of the former Royal Canadian Navy Mackenzie class destroyer escort HMCS *Saskatchewan*, which was sent to the bottom on 14 June 1997.

The *Saskatchewan* was built and launched by the Victoria Machinery Depot Company (hull and superstructure) and completed by Yarrow Ltd of Esquimalt, location of the main Pacific base of the Royal Canadian Navy (now called the Canadian Forces Maritime Command). The ship was commissioned on 16 February 1963. She was 112m (366ft) long, with a 13m (42ft) beam and a displacement of 2,900 tonnes (fully loaded). She had a top speed of 28 knots, a complement of 230 officers and men, and was armed with two 76mm (3 inch) guns, as well as mortars and homing torpedoes. The vessel was named after the Saskatchewan River and was the second of the Mackenzie-class destroyer escorts to enter service. She transited the Panama Canal twice in 1963, made four Atlantic crossings and participated in a major NATO exercise. The *Saskatchewan* eventually relieved HMCS *Nipigon* as flagship of the (NATO) Standing Naval Force Atlantic and served in the Pacific in a training capacity. She was decommissioned on 28 March 1994 and was due to be scrapped, when the ARSBC secured permission to carry out an environmental clean-up and to sink her as a dive attraction near Nanaimo, the principal 'hub' entry point for most visitors and divers to Vancouver Island.

HMCS *Saskatchewan* was the fifth ship (and the fourth destroyer) to be sunk as an artificial reef by the ARSBC. The sinking of the *Saskatchewan* was the first in a three-stage reef-creation effort off Nanaimo. (The second stage was achieved on 20 October 2001 at 12:40, with the sinking of the ex-HMS *Flamborough Head*.) After all hazardous materials had been removed, the final preparations for sinking involved flooding the engine room the day before to

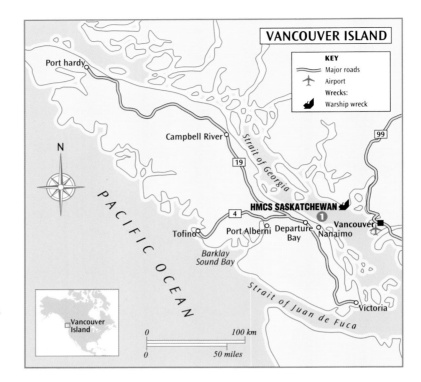

lower the ship's centre of gravity. Other preparatory work was undertaken to reduce the instability caused by air trapped below decks during the sinking. At 10:30 on 14 June 1997, members of the Royal Canadian Mounted Police bomb disposal unit cut the final holes. The *Saskatchewan* touched bottom approximately 3km (1¾ miles) off Nanaimo near the east side of Snake Island, which is located just a 10-minute boat ride from Nanaimo.

When you first dive down to the *Saskatchewan* the surface visibility appears generally poor due to the freshwater runoff from surrounding rivers. However, you soon pass through a colder thermocline, and although the surface waters cut down some of the light, the visibility on the wreck is usually excellent. The ship now lies almost upright with a slight list to port at a depth of 40m (130ft), completely intact and open for business. The bridge is at 20m (65ft), the top of the guns is at 26m (85ft) and the radar platform on the main mast is at 14m (45ft). Although

the vessel's paintwork still looks remarkably clean, the surface is now almost entirely covered by anemones, small sea urchins, scallops, tube worms, crinoids and, of course, countless numbers of rockfish. The bridge and deck spaces are all negotiable, and the railings and winch equipment are dotted with brightly coloured Plumose Anemones and sea stars.

This is one of the premier dive sites off eastern Vancouver Island and it should not be missed.

Above: The HMCS *Saskatchewan* has good visibility below the lower thermocline.

DESTINATION DIRECTORY

ATLANTIC OCEAN

CANADA – Bell Island

CLIMATE Conception Bay is fairly sheltered and has a micro climate that ensures fairly warm summers. However, this also means that when the warm air meets the cold Arctic waters, severe fog can clog the inlet for days at a time. This of course does not stop the diving, but can cut down on the ambient light.

BEST TIME TO GO June–September, when the icebergs from the north have calved and some of the smaller ones come into Conception Bay. The surface waters are warmest, and you can dive the wrecks and icebergs, and even snorkel with whales!

GETTING THERE Newfoundland is the most easterly province of Canada and, in fact, Cape Spear is the point of North America that is closest to Europe. Bell Island, the largest of three islands in Conception Bay, lies just west of St Johns, the provincial capital of Newfoundland, off the eastern seaboard of mainland Canada. There are daily commercial flights direct to St Johns from all the Canadian hub airports.

WATER TEMPERATURES There are several thermoclines in Conception Bay and these alter in intensity and depth depending on currents and prevailing winds. The water temperatures can be 0°C (32°F) at 30m (98ft) and as high as 15°C (59°F) at the surface.

DEPTH OF DIVES 25–42m (82–138ft).

RECOMPRESSION (HYPERBARIC) CHAMBERS Information not available.

DIVE PRACTICALITIES Advanced open water skills with some wreck skills are advisable but not necessary. There can be periodic current shifts and some surface swell in Conception Bay. The wrecks are all intact and divers can negotiate most aspects of them.

USA – East Coast
Northeast

CLIMATE The northeastern USA can have temperatures below freezing from November to April. North Carolina is located in a warm temperate zone where it is seasonal but moderate. January averages 7°C (45°F) and August can reach 36°C (97°F).

BEST TIME TO GO All wrecks are best dived in the northern summer, but the North Atlantic can get really rough.

GETTING THERE The northern wreck dives are reached from various towns and cities, including Atlantic City, New Jersey, New York and Massachusetts. North Carolina wreck sites are similarly reached from various towns and cities, including Morehead City, Beaufort, Wilmington and Hatteras.

WATER TEMPERATURE In the north, bottom temperatures on wrecks such as the *Andrea Doria* can be as low as 7°C (45°F) and rarely rise above 15°C (59°F) in late summer. Off North Carolina the range is from 13°C (55°F) in winter and spring, rising to 26°C (79°F) in late summer.

DEPTH OF DIVES The northern wrecks range from relatively shallow to quite deep, and some exceed depths of 60m (200ft). Most of the popular North Carolina wrecks are situated in the 24–46m (80–150ft) range.

RECOMPRESSION (HYPERBARIC) CHAMBERS There are several on the mainland of the USA.

DIVE PRACTICALITIES The northern wrecks are for very experienced divers only. The other wrecks can be enjoyed by most divers though the deeper ones require more training.

Florida Keys

CLIMATE Caribbean-like, the Florida Keys are sub-tropical with temperatures of 18–23°C (65–73°F) in winter and up to 30°C (86°F) in late summer. Most rainfall is concentrated between May and October, and at sea the wind gives a cooling breeze. The hurricane season formally begins on 1 June and ends on 30 November. However, historically, the chances of hurricane activity are greater between 15 August and 1 October.

BEST TIME TO GO All the year round, but the hurricane season can be a problem.

GETTING THERE International and domestic flights to Miami.

WATER TEMPERATURE Ranges from 22°C (72°F) from December to March, up to 29°C (84°F) from April to November.

DEPTH OF DIVES The maximum depth of the *Bibb* is 40m (131ft), the *Duane* 37m (120ft) and the *Spiegel Grove* 40m (130ft).

RECOMPRESSION (HYPERBARIC) CHAMBERS There are many in Florida – your diving operator will know the one that is the most suitable; or contact the Divers Alert Network.

DIVE PRACTICALITIES The *Duane* and the *Spiegel Grove* can be enjoyed by most divers, but the deeper dives, such as the *Bibb*, require more training.

BERMUDA

CLIMATE Bermuda is sub-tropical with temperatures of 18–23°C (65–73°F) in winter and up to 30°C (86°F) in late summer. The hurricane season is June to November, but most hurricanes occur from August to October.

BEST TIME TO GO Best dived in the northern summer, but the hurricane season is a problem. Bermuda can be dived all year round and has wrecks all around the islands so there will be leeward diving somewhere in most weathers.

GETTING THERE Bermuda can be reached directly by flights from Europe or indirectly via the USA.

WATER TEMPERATURE Ranges from 20°C (68°F) in January to 27°C (81°F) in August.

DEPTH OF DIVES Most wrecks are shallow, generally less than 30m (98ft).

RECOMPRESSION (HYPERBARIC) CHAMBERS Hyperbaric and Wound Care Department, King Edward VII Memorial Hospital, PO Box HM 1023, Hamilton, HM DX, Bermuda. Tel: +1 441 236 2345, ext 1896.

DIVE PRACTICALITIES Bermuda has always had a look-but-do-not-touch policy towards diving on wrecks. Now that legislation has transferred ownership of Bermuda's wrecks from the British Crown to the Bermudian Government a local wreck 'curator' has a similar role to that of the British Receiver of Wreck.

BAHAMAS

CLIMATE Typical Caribbean weather, but with a lower humidity than central Caribbean destinations due to the constant trade winds. Temperatures reach as high as 35°C (95°F) in the summer months.

BEST TIME TO GO The Bahamas are a year-round diving destination, but the hurricane season is usually from June to October, with increased wave height. Theo's Wreck is located offshore and the surface conditions may be choppy.

GETTING THERE Grand Bahama Island is the fourth largest of the Bahamas islands and is located in the northern Bahamas group, virtually opposite Miami. Theo's Wreck is the most westerly of the wrecks and is found due south of the capital, Freeport. Direct flights are available from all of the US hub airports, as well as a number of other Caribbean islands. Bahamasair runs a regular service between New Providence and Grand Bahama Island to connect with the international flights.

WATER TEMPERATURES From 23°C (74°F) in winter to 30°C (86°F) in summer.

DEPTH OF DIVES 25–33m (82–108ft).

RECOMPRESSION (HYPERBARIC) CHAMBERS The Bahamas Hyperbaric Centre, The Lyford Cay Hospital, Nassau, Bahamas. Tel: +1 242 362 4025; Chamber, tel: +1 242 362 5765.

DIVE PRACTICALITIES Advanced open water skills with some wreck skills are advisable but not necessary. This is a deep wreck and it is very easy to overstay your welcome here, particularly if you explore under the stern, so take care with your time in the water. Keep clear of any of the ship's handrails as these are covered in stinging hydroids.

BRITISH VIRGIN ISLANDS

CLIMATE Temperatures range from 18°C (64°F) in the winter months to 30°C (86°F) in the summer.

BEST TIME TO GO The British Virgin Islands have a fairly equable climate all year round. There is a hurricane risk from August to December, but it is rare for this to have an adverse affect on your holiday.

GETTING THERE East of Puerto Rico in the Leeward Island group, the British Virgin Islands comprise some 50 islands and cays (pronounced 'keys') and are the remains of a huge subterranean mountain plateau that rose millennia ago. The main channel separating the island chain was named after Sir Francis Drake, who sailed through the islands in 1585 on his way to conquering Hispaniola. It is the main connecting waterway between the Atlantic Ocean and the Caribbean Sea. The islands' geographical position probably contributes the most to the diversity of marine life around them. The wreck of the RMS *Rhone* is located off Salt Island, to the east of Tortola. There are regular flights from all the American hub airports, as well as flights from London Gatwick, operated by British Airways. However, due to the size of the international airport on Beef Island in the British Virgin Islands, all flights are first routed through San Juan in Puerto Rico. This involves American immigration procedures, collection of luggage and transfer to another terminal to catch the connecting flight with American Airlines (American Eagle) to Beef Island, which is connected to Tortola. Beef Island International Airport is quite small and you cannot get help with your luggage until you clear customs.

WATER TEMPERATURES From 21°C (70°F) in winter to 28°C (82°F) in the summer.

DEPTH OF DIVES 6–27m (20–89ft).

RECOMPRESSION (HYPERBARIC) CHAMBERS Nearest hyperbaric chamber is in San Juan: Puerto Rico Medical Center, Administracion de Servicios Medicos de Puerto Rico, Hyperbaric Chamber. Tel: +1 787 777 3535, ext. 6475.

DIVE PRACTICALITIES Due to the varying depths on both sections of the ship, it is perfectly suited for all levels of diver. The stern section is particularly favoured as a night dive. Strong currents can whip the sand up into the water column and there can be a heavy plankton bloom around April time, which can further reduce the visibility.

CAYMAN ISLANDS

CLIMATE Usually have a high humidity of 60 per cent and higher all year round. Temperatures can get as high as 35°C (95°F) in the summer months, but this is usually tempered by the almost constant trade winds from a southeasterly direction. Winters are warm with less wind and often have the best diving. Heavy rain should be expected in July and August.

BEST TIME TO GO The Cayman Islands are an all-year-round destination. The hurricane season is from June to October, and while there is a high probability of getting some rough weather, on the whole the islands are calm and sunny all year round.

GETTING THERE The Cayman Islands are located in the central Caribbean Sea 323km (200 miles) northwest of Jamaica and 194km (120 miles) south of Cuba. The shipwrecks are found all around the coasts of all three islands. The islands are serviced by direct flights from all of the United States hub airports as well as from London Heathrow. Many other international flights reroute through Miami.

WATER TEMPERATURES Can drop as low as 23°C (73°F) in January/February, but in the main the water stays around 28°C (82°F), with only occasional rises during hurricane season.

DEPTH OF DIVES 1–50m (40 in–164ft), although most of the best wrecks are in less than 15m (49ft) and many can be snorkelled.

RECOMPRESSION (HYPERBARIC) CHAMBERS Cayman Hyperbaric Services, PO Box 1675GT, Grand Cayman, B.W.I. Tel: +1 345 949 2989, e-mail: diveraid@candw.ky

DIVE PRACTICALITIES The wrecks are suitable for all levels of diver. Some are weather dependent and dive shops will choose the best and the safest wreck to suit the weather and your skills. All the wrecks in the Cayman Islands are protected and no one is allowed to remove any objects from them. During the spring, between Mother's Day and Father's Day, a local phenomenon known as 'sea itch' occurs. This is actually the microscopic planktonic stage of a jellyfish and can result in a condition similar to being stung by fire coral. A full suit should be worn during these weeks.

GRENADA
CLIMATE Temperatures vary between 24°C (75°F) and 29°C (85°F) and are usually equable, but strong winds and excessive rainfall should be expected in the summer months. The island averages over 1.27m (50in) of rain per year.

BEST TIME TO GO Grenada is a year-round diving destination, but summer is usually best, despite the fact that this is also the hurricane season.

GETTING THERE Grenada is the most southerly of the Windward Islands group and is surprisingly close to the mainland of South America. It is part of an active volcanic chain of islands, quite rugged in nature, and most of the diving only takes place on the sheltered western (Caribbean) side of the island. The *Bianca C* is found to the northwest of the airport. Grenada's Point Salinas International Airport is located in the southwestern tip of the

island and is reached daily by regular flights from the USA and Europe.

WATER TEMPERATURES From 23°C (73°F) in winter to 30°C (86°F) in summer.

DEPTH OF DIVES 33–50m (108–164ft).

RECOMPRESSION (HYPERBARIC) CHAMBERS There is no hyperbaric chamber on the island, although chambers are found in both Trinidad and Barbados, just 45 minutes away by low-flying emergency service. Contact Grenada Ministry of Health for the helplines. Tel: +1 473 440 2649.

DIVE PRACTICALITIES Experienced, advanced open water skills, with some wreck skills, are essential for this dive. An almost constant current sweeps this massive wreck and, because of its huge size, you tend not to stray too far from the shot line to allow for ease of making your way back to the surface.

HONDURAS
CLIMATE Very similar to the Cayman Islands, with high humidity and blistering hot days in summer, and sub-tropical in description. There is less wind in these regions, but there is a greater chance of rain coming in from the mainland. Average temperatures are around 28°C (82°F) all year round.

BEST TIME TO GO Honduras is a year-round dive destination and is generally considered to be at the edge of the hurricane zone. There is, however, more wind during summer.

GETTING THERE The island of Guanaja is located in the Bay Islands group of islands north of mainland Honduras in Central America. The *Jado Trader* is located southeast of South West Cay to the south of Guanaja. The islands are reached by various national and international airline companies from all of Central America and the main 'hub' airports of the US. Most visitors to the *Jado Trader* either arrive by day boat from one of the local hotel resorts or by live-aboard dive boat.

WATER TEMPERATURES From 23°C (73°F) in winter to 30°C (86°F) in summer.

DEPTH OF DIVES 26–34m (85–112ft).

RECOMPRESSION (HYPERBARIC) CHAMBERS Anthony's Key Resort, Hyperbaric Chamber, Roatan, Bay Island, Honduras. Tel: +504 45 10 49; e-mail: cms@globalnet.hn

DIVE PRACTICALITIES Suitable for most levels of diver, but advanced open water skills with some wreck skills are recommended due to the depth.

THE DUTCH ANTILLES
CLIMATE Sunshine on most days except in December–February; constant trade winds produce an arid desert climate, with August–October being the hottest months. The lowest temperatures are around 24°C (75°F) and the hottest rarely above 32°C (90°F), the average being 28°C (82°F), with a cooling breeze.

BEST TIME TO GO The islands of Aruba,

Bonaire and Curaçao are outside the hurricane belt. The protected leeward coasts allow diving all year. The more exposed sites are best dived in the summer and autumn.

GETTING THERE KLM Dutch Airways flies direct from Amsterdam, with connections all over Europe. Various airlines have connections from several North American and Latin American gateways to Aruba and Curaçao, with further connections between Aruba and Bonaire. Local airlines connect Curaçao and Bonaire. BonairExel also connects with St Maarten. American Eagle now has a connection between Puerto Rico's San Juan and Bonaire, while Air Jamaica connects Bonaire and Curaçao.

WATER TEMPERATURE The water temperature is 24°C (75°F) in the cool season, but averages 27°C (80°F).

DEPTH OF DIVES Often shallow – generally less than 40m (131ft).

RECOMPRESSION (HYPERBARIC) CHAMBERS There are no recompression facilities in Aruba. Patients are transferred to Curaçao, where the Saint Elisabeth Hospital (St Elisabeth Gasthuis) houses the island's two hyperbaric chambers. St Elisabeth Hospital, tel: +599 9462 5100/4900; recompression chamber, tel: +599 9462 7457. The Bonaire facility is at Saint Franciscus (Francisco) Hospital, Kaya Soeur Bartola, Kralendijk. Tel: +599 717 8900.

DIVE PRACTICALITIES Dive operators can organize suitable vehicles for shore diving, but you should not leave valuables in unattended vehicles. Some shore dives on Curaçao are accessed from private property where there is an entry charge. Recently on Bonaire, thieves have started stealing fuel from vehicles. In Aruba the *Atlantis VI* submarine and the *Seaworld Explorer* semi-submarine get very close to some wrecks, so divers should keep a careful lookout for them when underwater and when surfacing.

GREAT BRITAIN AND REPUBLIC OF IRELAND
England and Republic of Ireland
CLIMATE An island climate with four seasons, but very changeable. May to September are best. Autumn and winter are not good for diving, but you can dive from October to April in inland or other sheltered areas. Air temperatures are affected by the wind-chill factor. Most divers use dry suits all year round.

BEST TIME TO GO All year round in sheltered waters, but May to September if diving offshore. The high sun in summer allows more light to penetrate into the water.

GETTING THERE Due to the good system of international and domestic flights, roads and ferries, all sites can be reached easily.

WATER TEMPERATURE Highest in late summer with a range of 9–18°C (48–65°F). In winter it is 2–8°C (36–46°F). The west

coast tends to be the warmest due to the Gulf Stream.

DEPTH OF DIVES From the surface to deeper than recreational divers can dive on air. Technical diving is becoming popular on deeper wrecks.

RECOMPRESSION (HYPERBARIC) CHAMBERS There are many recompression (hyperbaric) chambers in the UK (www.ukdiving.co.uk/information/ hyperbaric.htm has a full list). Most are near the coast, but there are others inland, being used to treat disorders not connected with diving.

DIVE PRACTICALITIES Most dives require knowledge of tides and should be performed at slack water. Be prepared for the weather to deteriorate quickly. When diving with a commercial operator, respect the decisions of the captain, who knows and understands the local conditions.

Scotland – Scapa Flow
CLIMATE The weather is variable due to its exposed northern location. Susceptible to fog in early summer months as the land warms up, while the sea is still cold at 7°C (45°F).

BEST TIME TO GO Any time of the year is good, but space on dive boats gets limited during the UK holiday seasons: around Easter; the end of May Bank Holiday; July and August. Hotels and guesthouses are also busy at these times.

GETTING THERE The Orkney Islands are just 9.5 km (6 miles) off the north coast of Scotland. Scapa Flow is the large natural harbour in the southern Orkney Islands virtually surrounded by the mainland to the north, the islands of Hoy and Flotta to the south and west and Lamb Holm, Glims Holm, Burray and South Ronaldsay to the south and east. The wrecks are dotted all over Scapa Flow, with blockships found in the extreme east and west of the Flow, and the German light cruisers and battleships found roughly in the centre, arranged in a horseshoe shape around a rocky pinnacle called the Barrel of Butter. There is a regular ferry service from Scrabster (just north of Thurso along the A9) that sails to Stromness in northwestern Scapa Flow. Regular air services by British Airways and operated by Loganair operate daily from Edinburgh and Glasgow to connect with any international flights. Live-aboard and dive boats sail to the wrecks daily.

WATER TEMPERATURES 6°C (43°F) in the winter months of December through to February, to 15°C (59°F) in the summer months of August to September.

DEPTH OF DIVES 3–15m (10–50ft) on the blockships east; 12–18m (40–60ft) on the blockships west; and 15–42m (50–140ft) for the light cruisers and battleships.

RECOMPRESSION (HYPERBARIC) CHAMBERS The nearest hyperbaric chamber is the Orkney Hyperbaric Unit, Old Academy, Back Road, Stromness, Orkney. Tel: 01856 888000. More serious cases will be referred to the Hyperbaric Medicine Unit,

Aberdeen Royal Infirmary, Foresterhill, Aberdeen, AB25 2ZB, Scotland, UK. Tel: 0845 408 6008.

DIVE PRACTICALITIES From beginner to the most advanced and qualified technical divers. Scapa Flow can be as complicated or as easy as you want to make it. In fact, many divers get their first open water diving experience on a shipwreck in Scapa Flow. There can be current at the end of the dive on the blockships of Burra Sound, and depth- and time-related problems on the deeper wrecks resulting in possible decompression sickness. For the most part the diving is in open water, jumping off the side of a dive boat and swimming down a shot line in generally poor visibility in dark water. The shipwrecks in Scapa Flow have, for the most part, been deteriorating steadily since 1919, and extreme caution should be exercised when approaching the ships. Penetration is *not* recommended for anyone. Diving the blockships of Burra Sound can only be done in slack water before the flooding tide, to allow for the maximum time at depth in slack water so that divers can be swept gently into Scapa Flow at the end of the dive and not out to sea.

Scotland – SS Hispania

CLIMATE Usually wet and windy, and air temperatures are affected by the warm waters of the North Atlantic drift. Fog is common in the summer months, but air temperatures can reach as high as 28°C (82°F) in the summer.

BEST TIME TO GO The wreck can be dived all year round, but it should only be dived at slack water, as the current in this section of the Sound of Mull can be fierce, rendering the wreck undiveable.

GETTING THERE The wreck of the SS *Hispania* is located off Sgeir Mor on the east coast of the Isle of Mull, in the northern aspects of the Sound of Mull. Her general position lies facing towards the shore, and she is close to a red channel buoy. Oban is the main town in the area and is a travel hub for exploring the Western Isles of Scotland. It can be reached by road or rail with direct links to Edinburgh and Glasgow, where both international and domestic flights are catered for.

WATER TEMPERATURES Water temperature can range from 14°C (57°F) in August and September, down to as low as 5°C (41°F) in January and February.

DEPTH OF DIVES 15–30m (49–98ft).

RECOMPRESSION (HYPERBARIC) CHAMBER Dunstaffnage Marine Laboratory, Dunbeg, Oban, PA37 1QA. Website: www.sams.ac.uk/commercial/srsl/diving/diving.htm

DIVE PRACTICALITIES A minimum of advanced open water with some wreck skill is required, and PADI Mutilevel and PADI Wreck Diver Qualifications are preferred. However, many novice divers have dived this superb wreck accompanied by

experienced dive guides and instructors on a one-to-one basis. In midsummer there can be large stinging jellyfish. Their stinging tentacles sometimes get caught on the shot line or on the wreck itself, so care should be taken to avoid these.

SOUTH AFRICA

CLIMATE In summer the southeasterly 'Cape Doctor' blows daily. The temperatures on land average 30°C (86°F), but the water temperatures can drop to as low as 7°C (45°C). In winter a northwesterly wind hammers Table Bay's shipping. Winter is the rainy season in the Cape and although the air temperature range is 10–17°C (50–63°F), water temperatures can maintain an even 14–16°C (57–61°F).

BEST TIME TO GO All year round, although the surface conditions are obviously seasonal and the diving varies. The best time to dive the Atlantic is November to March, and the best time to dive Table Bay is June and July.

GETTING THERE South Africa has many international flights, but once there visitors require either a shuttle service or to rent private transport, as public services are not adequate. All asphalt roads are in good condition.

WATER TEMPERATURE Atlantic: 6–18°C (43–64°F); False Bay: 8–22°C (46–72°F).

DEPTH OF DIVES From the surface to 65m (213ft) on the continental shelf and deeper for technical diving.

RECOMPRESSION (HYPERBARIC) CHAMBERS In Cape Town there are four decompression chambers available: UCT Oceanographic department, tel: +27 21 650 3277; Claremont Hospital, tel: +27 21 670 4300; Cape Diving and Salvage (Cape Town Harbour), tel: +27 21 448 4341; SA Navy (Simons Town). DAN South Africa is available to registered divers.

DIVE PRACTICALITIES The Cape of Storms can be very unforgiving and it is always best to visit any new location with a local dive guide. There are various operators specializing in all levels of diver. Most divers in Cape Town use a 7mm (¼ inch) wetsuit with hood, but dry suits are becoming more popular.

MEDITERRANEAN SEA

MALTA

CLIMATE The island's position in the central Mediterranean makes it susceptible to seasonal winds from virtually every direction. Although the island appears arid due to the rock base being so porous, it does get heavy prolonged rain showers in August and September. Air temperatures vary from 11°C (52°F) in the winter to over 35°C (95°F) in the summer, but there is very little humidity.

BEST TIME TO GO Malta is a year-round destination and, while there can be periodic winter storms, there is always a lee shore and you are still able to dive on any

number of wrecks. It is obviously quieter in the winter months and the water is cooler. All the main diving centres offer a full service including Trimix and Nitrox.

GETTING THERE The Maltese archipelago is located some 93km (58 miles) south of Sicily and 455km (282 miles) from the African coast. Geographically and politically isolated, the Republic of Malta consists of three main islands, Malta, Gozo and Comino, and a number of smaller satellite islands. Air Malta provides a high level of service from a large number of airports all over the world and, in particular, many European cities. From the UK there are direct flights from Glasgow, Manchester, Birmingham, Dublin, London Heathrow and Gatwick. A large number of other carriers also fly direct to Luqa Airport on Malta, and there is a helicopter service between Malta and Gozo. However, most people drive north to the ferry terminal at Cirkewwa and cross by ferry to Mgarr harbour on Gozo: this journey time is only around 25 minutes. The dive centres either arrange your shore diving or have a boat to take you to the offshore wrecks.

WATER TEMPERATURES 14°C (57°F) in the winter to 25°C (77°F) in the summer months.

DEPTH OF DIVES 25–60m (82–197ft), so be careful of your depth.

RECOMPRESSION (HYPERBARIC) CHAMBERS Both Gozo and Malta have hyperbaric hospital facilities. In any medical emergency, there is a helicopter service with direct links to the police and the nearest hospital. All decompression accidents are ferried in this way. Emergency, tel: 196; Hyperbaric Unit, tel: +356 2123 4766.

DIVE PRACTICALITIES There are dives suitable for all levels of diver, but advanced open water level is recommended due to the depth and conditions. Divers should have some wreck experience. Local fishermen are resentful of divers when shore diving, since they believe that divers scare away the fish. They have been known to throw stones, hit divers with fishing rods and throw access ladders into the sea. Do not leave your rental car with equipment visible inside, because it may not be there when you get back!

CYPRUS

CLIMATE Temperate; long, hot, dry summers and cool winters, with sunshine on most days. Average temperatures can rise to 32°C (90°F) in summer with a cooling breeze, and drop to 17°C (63°F) in winter.

BEST TIME TO GO All year round, but May–December is best. A thick semi-dry suit is recommended in the spring, and a 5mm (0.2 inch) one in the summer and autumn; a dry suit is best from January to April.

GETTING THERE There are many scheduled and charter flights from major European gateways.

WATER TEMPERATURE The water temperature is 18–24°C (65–75°F).

DEPTH OF DIVES 16–43m (53–141ft).

RECOMPRESSION CHAMBERS Larnaka General Hospital – Hyperbaric Center. Tel: +357 24 63 03 22. Dive In Larnaca has its own recompression facility. Website: www.dive-in.com.cy

DIVE PRACTICALITIES Remember that several divers have died while penetrating this vessel.

RED SEA

EGYPT

CLIMATE It is warm and mostly dry in winter, with an average temperature of 20°C (70°F), but cold and windy out at sea. A dry suit, semi-dry suit or thick wetsuit is preferable. It is hot and dry in summer, with an average temperature of 35°C (95°F), but the winds at sea can be strong. Wetsuits are fine, but it is wise to have warm clothes available on a boat.

BEST TIME TO GO All year round, but best in summer, May to September. High season for bookings is October to April.

GETTING THERE There are international airports at Râs el Naqb (Naqb is also spelt Naqab and Naqeb) to serve Taba and Nuweiba, Râs Nusrâni (called Sharm el Sheikh Airport), south of Hurghada for Hurghada and Marsa 'Alam. There is a smaller airport at El Gouna.

WATER TEMPERATURE Averages 25°C (77°F) in summer, 19°C (66°F) in winter.

DEPTH OF DIVES From the surface to depths well beyond the accepted limits of sport or recreational technical diving.

RECOMPRESSION (HYPERBARIC) CHAMBERS There are recompression chambers at Dahab next to the Dahabeya Hotel. Emergency number (9:30–6pm), tel: 069 364 0536; 24-hour emergency number, tel: 010 143 3325. At Sharm el Sheikh opposite the naval harbour – Hyperbaric Medical Center, tel: 20 62 660 922/3; fax: 20 62 661 011; e-mail: hyper_med_center@ sinainet.com.eg mailto: hyper_med_center@ sinainet.com.eg. The El Gouna Hospital north of Hurghada, tel: 20 12 187550 or 20 65 549709. The Naval Hospital Hurghada, tel: 20 65 449 150. Safâga, for emergencies or for further information, contact either Dr Hanaa, tel: 012 219 0383 or Dr Hossam, tel: 012 218 7550 and North of Marsa 'Alam in Ecolodge Shagra Village at Marsa Shagra, tel: +195 100262.

DIVE PRACTICALITIES Visibility is at least 20m (66ft) on fringing or nearshore reefs, except near ports and where divers or currents stir up the silt. About 30–40m (98–131ft) is common over deep water. Have good buoyancy control and wear some form of protective clothing against sunburn, fire coral and stinging hydroids; at night there is an extra problem with lionfish. Ear infections are common: they are often caused by a fungus, so use an ear-drying agent after each dive and an anti-fungal agent to treat them.

SUDAN

CLIMATE It is warm and dry in winter, but then the offshore winds can be very strong. It is wise to have warm clothes on the boat. In summer it can be unpleasantly hot on land, with temperatures of 47°C (117°F), while at sea the temperature is comfortable but humid. Thin wetsuits are best in winter, but Lycra Skins are fine in summer.

BEST TIME TO GO All year round. Most live-aboard boats operating out of Port Sudan only do so in the winter, but it can get very windy and rough at that time. The best time to go is in May–July and September. Avoid August, when heavy rain in nearby Ethiopia causes south winds, Haboobs and generally poor weather.

GETTING THERE It is best to get an international flight via Cairo to Port Sudan, rather than arriving at Khartoum, as the connecting flights to Port Sudan are subject to delays.

WATER TEMPERATURE Averages 28°C (82°F) in summer, 27°C (81°F) in winter.

DEPTH OF DIVES From the surface to depths well beyond the accepted limits of sport or recreational technical diving.

RECOMPRESSION (HYPERBARIC) CHAMBERS None.

DIVE PRACTICALITIES Visibility is at least 20m (66ft) on fringing or nearshore reefs, except near ports and where divers or currents stir up the silt. About 30–40m (98–131ft) is common over deep water. Have good buoyancy control and wear some form of protective clothing against sunburn, fire coral and stinging hydroids. At night there is an extra problem with lionfish. Ear infections are common: they are often caused by a fungus, so use an ear-drying agent after each dive and use an anti-fungal agent to treat them.

INDIAN OCEAN

AUSTRALIA – West Coast
HMAS Swan

CLIMATE Southern coastal regions of Western Australia are mild and sunny. Temperatures average between 32°C (90°F) in the warm, dry summer (December–February) and 14°C (57°F) in the wet, mild winter (June–August).

BEST TIME TO GO October to May, especially January to March.

GETTING THERE Tours run from the town of Dunsborough, heading out 2.4km (1¼ nautical miles) off Point Piquet, Meelup Beach, into the Bay. Location: Geographe Bay, Western Australia.

WATER TEMPERATURE 17–22°C (63–72°F).

DEPTH OF DIVES 30m (98ft).

RECOMPRESSION (HYPERBARIC) CHAMBER Fremantle, 255km (158 miles). Fremantle Hospital, Alma Street, Fremantle, Western Australia 6160. Tel: +08 9431 3333. A diver suffering decompression illness in the north of the state will be flown to nearby Perth by the Royal Flying Doctor Service.

DIVE PRACTICALITIES The wreck is diver-friendly, but penetration requires appropriate qualifications. Minimum 5mm (0.2 inch) wetsuit recommended for warmth. Suitable for beginner to advanced divers.

HMAS Perth

CLIMATE Southern coastal regions of Western Australia are mild and sunny. Temperatures average between 32°C (90°F) in the warm, dry summer (December–February) and 14°C (57°F) in the wet, mild winter (June–August).

BEST TIME TO GO March to November. The most predictable conditions are during March, April and May, while the best visibility and numbers of passing whales occur during June, July and August. The bay suffers from intermittent bad weather in that period. Divers can expect poor, surgy conditions brought about by easterly swells in December, January and February.

GETTING THERE Tours run from the town of Albany, leaving from the main jetty, and also from the pristine white beach of Frenchmans Bay. A double dive can be completed in four hours, with some operators taking a lunch break on the beach. Location: King George Sound, Albany, Western Australia.

DEPTH OF DIVES 35m (100ft).

WATER TEMPERATURE March to May 20–22°C (72–68°F), June to August and November 18°C (64°F), September and October 16°C (61°F).

RECOMPRESSION (HYPERBARIC) CHAMBER Fremantle, 409km (254 miles). Fremantle Hospital, Alma Street, Fremantle, Western Australia 6160. Tel: +08 9431 3333. A diver suffering decompression illness in the north of the state will be flown to nearby Perth by the Royal Flying Doctor Service.

DIVE PRACTICALITIES Visibility is 5–20m (48–64ft). The wreck is diver friendly with cut-outs across the ship. Many internal areas have direct, vertical access to the surface. Minimum 5mm (0.2 inch) wetsuit recommended for warmth. Suitable for beginner to advanced divers.

PACIFIC OCEAN

MALAYSIA

CLIMATE Tropical, warm and humid all year with average temperatures of 26–30°C (80–86°F); rarely below 20°C (68°F), except on high ground. Monsoon winds influence the climate, but strong winds are rare. Typhoons miss this region by several hundred kilometres, thus Borneo is called 'the land below the wind'. Only in the north of Peninsular Malaysia's east coast does tourism need to close during the monsoon season.

BEST TIME TO GO Each area has two main seasons, one drier and the other the monsoon season, although in Malaysia this is more aptly called the wetter season. However, the wreck dives in mainland Borneo can be dived all year round.

HOW TO GET THERE To reach Peninsular Malaysia fly to Kuala Lumpur, then take domestic flights onwards. However, many live-aboard boats offering technical diving depart from Singapore, so you can fly directly to Singapore. To visit East Malaysia fly to Kota Kinabalu, and then carry on by domestic flight, ferry or road.

WATER TEMPERATURES 25°C (77°F) over deep water in the cooler season, 31°C (88°F) in warm season; 30°C (86°F) in shallow water.

DEPTH OF DIVES From the surface to depths greater than sport or recreational technical divers should dive, so act responsibly.

RECOMPRESSION (HYPERBARIC) CHAMBERS
■ Peninsular Malaysia at Lumut Naval Base, 32100, Lumut, Perak. Tel: +605 683 7090; website: www.hatl.gov.my/divemed.htm
■ Centre for Wound Care and Hyperbaric Medicine (Hyperbaric Health), 16, Persiaran Greentown 1, Greentown Business Centre, 30450 Ipoh, Perak. Tel: +605 242 6237; or +605 C-H-A-M-B-E-R www.hbomalaysia.com
■ Kuantan Naval Base, Tg. Gelang 25990 Kuantan, Pahang. Tel: +609 513 3333.
■ East Malaysia at Labuan, Pejabat Selam, Markas Wilayah Laut Dua, 87007 Labuan. Tel: +608 741 2122.
■ The Singapore Navy has recompression chambers in Singapore: Naval Medicine & Hyperbaric Centre. 24-hour emergency hotline, tel: +65 6758 1733.
■ Tan Tock Seng Hospital Hyperbaric Medicine Center, 11 Jalan Tan Tock Seng, Basement 1 Tan Tock Seng Hospital, 308433 Singapore. Tel: +65 6355 9021/22.

DIVE PRACTICALITIES Visibility approaches 60m (197ft) in good conditions and is rarely below 30m (98ft). In general the shallower wrecks do not have very strong currents, but those that are deep enough to require technical diving can have fierce currents.

THE PHILIPPINES

CLIMATE Tropical, with a temperature range of 23–36°C (73–97°F). There are pronounced seasons: the dry season is from November to February, while the wet season is from June to October, when typhoons can occur in the northern part of the country.

BEST TIME TO GO Year round for most areas, except in the far north. April and May are reliably calm throughout the archipelago; December to June is the peak season.

GETTING THERE Fly to either Ninoy Aquino International Airport (Manila), or Mactan International Airport (Cebu); then onward domestic flights to all major destinations. Many destinations now have good ferry services, which eases the cost of diver's weight problems when flying.

WATER TEMPERATURES 25°C (77°F) in the cooler season, to 31°C (88°F).

DEPTH OF DIVES From the surface to depths greater than sport or recreational technical divers should dive, so act responsibly.

RECOMPRESSION (HYPERBARIC) CHAMBERS Recompression chambers are available in many areas. Evacuation assistance can be obtained from AFP Search & Rescue Facilities in Metro Manila.
■ Subic Bay, Subic Bay Freeport Zone, SBMA Olongapo City. Tel: +63 47 2527952.
■ Manila, AFP Medical Center, V. Lunar Road, Quezon City. Tel: +63 2 9207183.
■ Cavite City, Sangley Recompression Chamber NSWG, Philippine Fleet, Naval Base Cavite, Sangley Point, Cavite City. Tel: +63 46 5242061.
■ Batangas City, St Patricks Hospital, Lopez Jaena St, Batangas City 4200. Tel: +63 43 7238388.
■ Cebu, VISCOM Station Hospital, Camp Lapu Lapu, Lahug, Cebu City. Tel: +63 32 310709.
■ Evacuation Assistance: AFP Search & Rescue Facilities, GHQ, Philippine Air Force. Villamor Air Base, Pasay City, Metro Manila. Tel: +63 2 9117996.

DIVE PRACTICALITIES All the wrecks mentioned here are in sheltered water. Visibility is generally excellent, with 40m+ (130ft+) on a flood tide.

CHUUK

CLIMATE Tropical; dry season between December and April; rainy season from April to December. Located on the southern edge of the typhoon belt, with occasionally severe damage. Temperature range is 29–32°C (85–90°F).

BEST TIME TO GO All year round, although photographers prefer January–April.

GETTING THERE Continental Airlines with routings through Guam and Honolulu.

WATER TEMPERATURE Ranges between 27°C (80°F) and 29°C (84°F).

DEPTH OF DIVES From the surface to deeper than recreational divers can dive on air. The best wrecks are in 21m (69ft) or less, but there are deeper wrecks for more advanced and technical divers.

RECOMPRESSION (HYPERBARIC) CHAMBERS Divers no longer have to go to Guam. The nearest operational recompression chamber is at Neauo Village in Weno, the capital island of Chuuk. Tel: 691 330 2318. It is owned by Hyperbaric Health Australia (www.hyperbarichealth.com) and operated by Bruton Enterprises.

DIVE PRACTICALITIES The level of experience required by the diver depends on the site.

VANUATU

CLIMATE Two seasons: summer (November–March), winter (April–October). Temperatures range from 23°C (73°F) to 28°C (82°F).

BEST TIME TO GO All year round.

GETTING THERE Fly from Sydney or Auckland to Port Villa on Éfaté and connect to Espiritu Santo.

WATER TEMPERATURE 25–30°C (77–86°F).

DEPTH OF DIVES 15–70m (49–230ft). If you

are not a technical diver, be careful of the maximum depth.

RECOMPRESSION (HYPERBARIC) CHAMBERS
ProMedical's facility in Port Vila, Éfaté, Vanuatu. Tel: +678 25566; website: www.promedical.com.vu

DIVE PRACTICALITIES Easier sections of the *President Coolidge* are suitable for all levels of diver, but penetration lengthwise and deep dives to the stern are only for technical divers or those who have a thorough understanding of decompression stops. For penetration, if you are not with a guide, tie a safety guideline from outside. Carry a powerful underwater light and a backup. Dives deeper than 50m (164ft) on air are beyond the depths recommended by most training agencies.

SOLOMON ISLANDS

CLIMATE Located just a few degrees below the equator, the Solomon Islands enjoy a year-round tropical climate moderated by the sea air. Daytime temperatures average around 29°C (84°F) with high humidity. Evenings may be as cool as 19°C (66°F). There are no defined seasons, but November to May are the wetter months when squalls and cyclones may occur.

BEST TIME TO GO Diving conditions are good at any time of the year, but the drier season runs from April through to December. There is no monsoon season. Rain can be expected at any time, but it usually blows over very quickly.

GETTING THERE International airport at Honiara receives flights from most major airlines via Australia and New Zealand. Regular internal flights to Gizo.

WATER TEMPERATURE Waters are warm and tropical with an average temperature of 27°C (80°F). Variations can occur due to changes in currents and the time of year.

DEPTH OF DIVES Varies according to dive site. Hellcat lies at 12m (39ft), average visibility 10–20m (32–65ft). *Toa Maru* is at 12–27m (39–89ft), average visibility 10–40m (32–131ft). *Kinugawa Maru* lies at 3–24m (10–80ft), average visibility 14–40m (46–131ft).

RECOMPRESSON (HYPERBARIC) CHAMBERS Nearest chamber is at ProMedical's facility in Port Vila, Éfaté, Vanuatu. The hyperbaric unit is available to treat diving illnesses on a 24-hour basis. Tel: +678 25566; website: www.promedical.com.vu

DIVE PRACTICALITIES Lycra suits or thin wetsuits are recommended. Take a comprehensive first-aid kid containing suitable medication for coral cuts, ear infections and gastrointestinal infections. Malaria medication is also strongly recommended. Operators will want to see log books and C-cards. Visitor permits for stays of up to 30 days are issued on arrival, provided visitors have proof of onward tickets and valid passports. Do not collect or touch any unexploded ammunitions.

MILNE BAY, PAPUA NEW GUINEA

CLIMATE Tropical. Southeast trade winds in May–November. Rainfall highly variable, with no well-defined wet season. Cyclones are rare because the area is too close to the equator.

BEST TIME TO GO October to June, avoiding strongest southeast trade winds.

GETTING THERE Milne Bay Province is situated at the southeast tip of the island of New Guinea. The capital is Alotau. Air Niugini flies to Port Moresby from Sydney, Brisbane, Cairns (daily), Singapore and Manila, and there are Air Niugini connecting flights from Port Moresby to Alotau on most days of the week. A 60-day tourist visa is available on arrival for 100 Kina (about US$30). Customs and immigration are friendly and courteous and understand about divers carrying a lot of gear. Air Niugini also has a generous excess baggage allowance for diving gear. It is a good idea to mention this when buying your ticket.

WATER TEMPERATURES Variable, but at the Blackjack site usually in a range of 27°C (80°F) in July/August to 29°C (84°F) during December/January.

DEPTH OF DIVES Maximum depth: 46m (151ft).

RECOMPRESSION (HYPERBARIC) CHAMBERS There is a recompression chamber at the Private Hospital and Clinic in Port Moresby, and a jet aircraft is available for emergency evacuations. There is also a recompression chamber being installed at the Tawali Resort in Milne Bay.

DIVE PRACTICALITIES Skill level required: advanced with deep diving experience. Current up to 1 knot (usually less). Possible decompression dive – keep half your breathing gas supply for the ascent. Safety stops essential.

AUSTRALIA – East Coast

CLIMATE Tropical, with southeast trade winds dominating between May and October, doldrums around April and November, and calm but risk of cyclones during months of January, February and March, which is the wet season.

BEST TIME TO GO The wreck is exposed to the weather. The best time to visit, with a high probability of a successful dive, is between October and June. There is a possibility of cyclones during the wet season months of January to March. July to September have a high probability of strong southeast trade winds, making the approach to the wreck impossible.

GETTING THERE The wreck of the *Yongala* is located in the central section of the Great Barrier Reef about 22km (12 nautical miles) west of Cape Bowling Green. Its closest access is through the city of Townsville, which can be reached by air or road from Cairns or Brisbane in Australia.

WATER TEMPERATURES Water temperatures can drop to lows of 22°C (72°F) in July, but usually rise to 27°C (80°F) or higher in January.

DEPTH OF DIVES Maximum depth: 28m (92ft).

RECOMPRESSION (HYPERBARIC) CHAMBERS A long-established hyperbaric treatment facility is located at the Townsville General Hospital.
Hyperbaric Unit, PO Box 670 Townsville, Queensland, Qld 4810. Tel: +61 07 4781 9211.

DIVE PRACTICALITIES Skill level: not suitable for beginners unless conditions are perfect. Current, rough surface conditions, offshore so no shelter, large marine life (groupers).

NEW ZEALAND

CLIMATE New Zealand has a maritime climate due to its small land mass. Prevailing winds are from the west all year so the east coast has calmer conditions, more suited to diving. Be prepared: the weather can change quickly at any time of the year. Air temperatures in the North Island are 15–25°C (59°–77°F) in summer and 9°–15°C (48–59°F) in winter. South Island temperatures are 10–22°C (50–72°F) in summer and 2–10°C (36–50°F) in winter.

BEST TIME TO GO Summer lasts from December to March and winter from June to August. Weather is generally mildest between February and June with warm, clear water.

GETTING THERE Auckland and Wellington International Airports receive flights from most of the world's major airlines. For the *Rainbow Warrior* fly to Auckland. Drive to Paihia in the Bay of Islands (approximately three hours). Dive shops run regular, well-organized trips. For the *Mikhail Lermontov* fly to Wellington. Take a ferry to Picton. Dive shops organize trips and transport. For Taioma, it is a three-hour drive or 40-minute internal flight from Auckland to Tauranga. Regular trips are run by local dive shops.

WATER TEMPERATURES Water temperatures vary seasonally between 14°C (57°F) and 23°C (73°F) in the north, 8°C (46°F) and 18°C (64°F) in the south.

RECOMPRESSION (HYPERBARIC) CHAMBERS Hyperbaric Units are sited at the Royal New Zealand Naval Hospital, Private Bag 32901, Devonport, Auckland, New Zealand. Tel: +64 09 445 5920; and at Christchurch Hyperbaric Medicine Unit, Private Bag 4710 Christchurch, New Zealand. Tel: +64 03 364 0045. In case of a dive accident, the Diver Emergency Number in New Zealand is 0800 4DES 111 (0800 4337 111).

DIVE PRACTICALITIES A 5mm (0.2 inch) wetsuit can be worn comfortably for northern summer diving, while a 7mm (¼ inch) or dry suit is recommended for year-round southern diving or winter diving in the North Island. Most shops rent gear. Certification cards will need to be shown to dive operators. It is recommended that you prebook diving during weekends and public holidays.

CANADA – Vancouver Island

CLIMATE Equable temperatures in the summer, usually around 25°C (77°F). Winters can be long, wet and windy, with temperatures plummeting below 0°C (32°F).

BEST TIME TO GO July–September after the spring thaw.

GETTING THERE Vancouver Island is located off the western shore of British Columbia. The wreck of HMCS *Saskatchewan* is located on the east coat of Vancouver Island near a group of small islands to the east of Nanaimo, the nearest major town. Vancouver is the nearest major airport, and many international airlines have direct flights into this gateway city. From Vancouver, most visitors travel by ferry to Nanaimo, which takes around 2½ hours. Local dive operators run regular trips out to the wreck and nearby seal colonies. The journey takes about 25 minutes.

WATER TEMPERATURES 5°C (41°F) in the winter to 15°C (59°F) in the summer.

DEPTH OF DIVES 25–32m (82–105ft).

RECOMPRESSION (HYPERBARIC) CHAMBERS The Vancouver General Hospital, Division of Hyperbaric Medicine, 855 West 12th Avenue, Vancouver, British Columbia, Canada V5Z 1M9. Tel (24 hours): +64 604 875 5000. Contact coastguard or police and emergency evacuation at Nanaimo, tel: 758 8181.

DIVE PRACTICALITIES A minimum of advanced open water with some wreck skills is required, and PADI Multilevel and PADI Wreck Diver Qualifications are preferred. As with all wreck diving, there is a chance that equipment may become snagged or even torn by a jagged piece of metal. Fortunately, due to the cold water in these parts deterioration on the wreck is very slow, so there are fewer jagged pieces than on typical shipwrecks. Time at depth is the other known problem, and all divers are advised to wear a diving computer and watch and tables as backup. A windbreaker is recommended for the journey back to shore, since there is a real danger of becoming chilled after the dive.

INDEX

PICTURE CREDITS

African Imagery/Andrew Woodburn 68; Andy Belcher 144, 147; Kevin Deacon/Ocean Earth Images 125, 128, 131, 132; Ecoscene/Reinhard Dirscherl 96; Stephen Frink 29; Gary Gentile Productions 26–7, 33, 57; Bob Halstead 136, 140, 143; Jack Jackson 48–9, 50–1, 98, 101, 112, 115, 116, 119; John Liddiard 149, 150, 153; Lochman Transparencies/Dr Geoff Taylor back cover, 104, 108–9; Jason Martin 34, 64, 67; Geri Murphy 6, 36, 40–41, 44, 122, 127; Oceans Image/Tony Baskeyfield 80, 82, 83; Ocean Image/Charles Hood front cover, 2, 10–11, 52, 86; Ocean Image/Simon Rogerson 1; PPL/Len Deeley 90, 91, 92–3, 94–5; Geoff Paynter 107; SeaPics.com/Amar Guillen 22; SeaPics.com/Bill Harrigan; Rick Stanley 18, 21; Lawson Wood/Ocean Eye Films 12–13, 30, 42, 46, 61, 63, 72, 76, 77, 78.